Every Woman's
GUIDE TO
Self Defence

Every Woman's GUIDE TO Self Defence

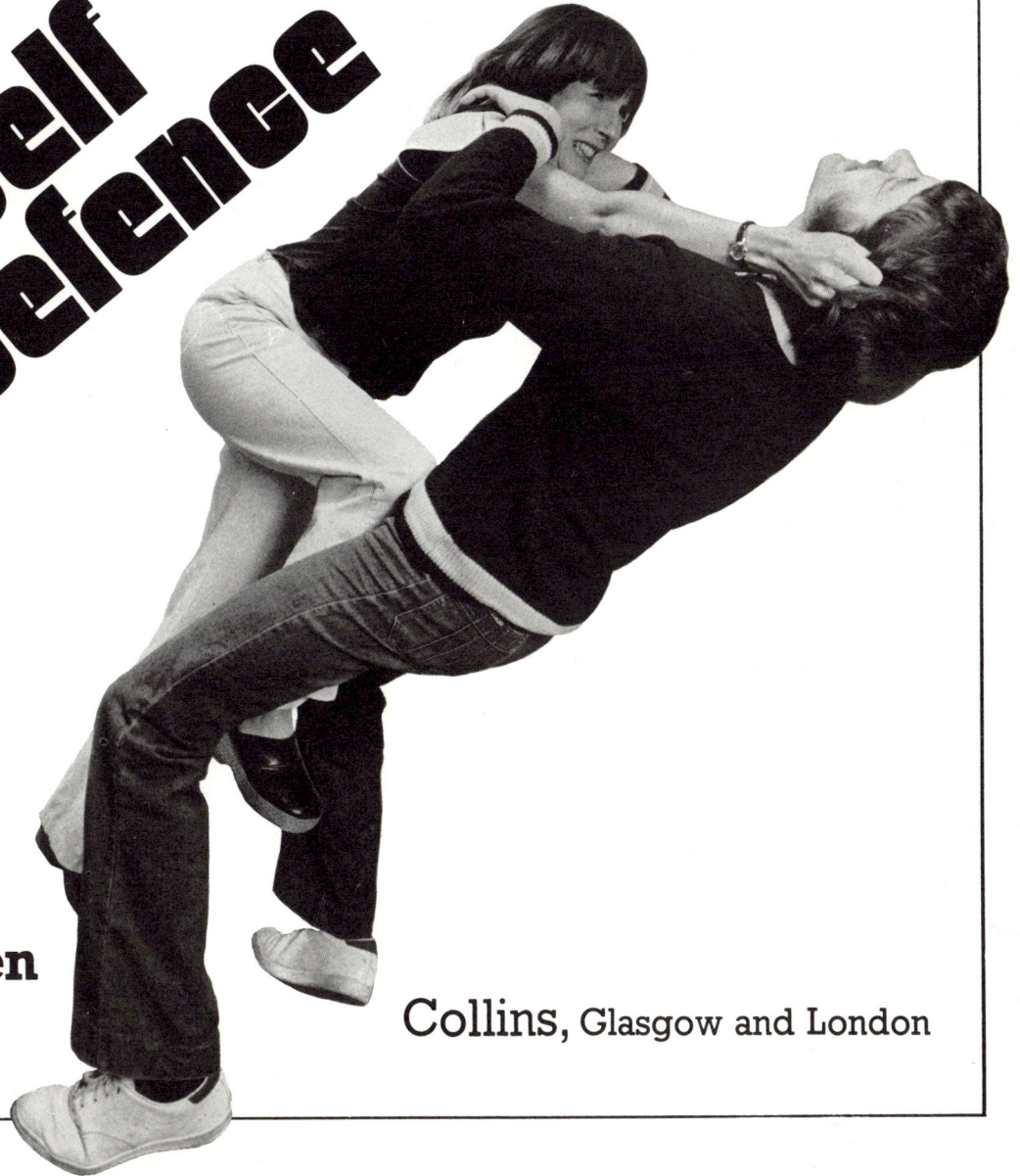

Kathleen Hudson

Collins, Glasgow and London

Published by Collins, Glasgow and London
First Published 1977
Copyright © Kathleen Hudson 1977

Design by Paul Fella

Drawings by Ron Lumsden

Photographs on pages 42, 43, 50, 51, 57, 58, 62,
63, 74, 75, 76, 77, 88, 89, 90
and 91 by Henry Redfern.
**Cover and all other
photographs by Conrad
Fisher, Peterloo Studios.**

Set in Optima
Printed in Great Britain
ISBN 0 00 435002 2 (paperback)
0 00 435003 0 (cased)

CONTENTS

Acknowledgements to M. Allingham, P. Fella,
L. Wiszniewski, S. Gamwell and to L. Wiszniewski
for technical advice received.

Preface

In these days of ever-increasing violence, self defence has become a necessary part of survival. Various Oriental martial arts offer instruction in self defence in their particular way in many different places throughout the country. Although quite effective, in order to be of use they require many hours of regular hard training spread over months or years. Many people find that the intensive training required would take too much time or energy, or both. Because of this some people do not bother to prepare themselves at all; others merely nibble at a given art forgetting that with the best of intentions a little knowledge is a dangerous thing.

I have written this book for all women. As a woman who has been in various situations I have observed that in most cases the attack on a woman is vastly different from usual acts of violence. The method of dealing with such situations must of necessity differ greatly from set defences prescribed by any sport practised by both sexes. You must apply the most effective and nearest weapon to the most available vulnerable point of your enemy. One has to consider the fact that any woman's body is generally physically weaker than that of any male. Females are usually more easily subdued because they panic and attempt to use their feeble strength against a man. Only *skill* can be successful against a stronger opponent.

Keeping this in mind I have described the most reasonable defences against set attacks which are based upon various techniques adapted from Atemi-Jitsu, Kung Fu, Ju-Jitsu and Judo. I am 159 cm/5 ft 2½ in tall and weigh just under 51 kilo/112 lb. My partner in most of the pictures is 216 cm/6 ft 1 in and weighs 92 kilo/203 lb. Against such obvious physical superiority only *skill* can prevail.

Most situations can be avoided by simply not

permitting them to arise. In most circumstances a sensible person knows when discretion becomes the better part of valour. Obvious examples include;

Don't encourage a male if you have no intention of playing.

Don't find yourself alone in a room with a suspicious character.

Don't walk down dark streets alone. If you must, keep away from doorways and openings.

Avoid sitting in empty train carriages. Seek people. The lone menace will not attack in a crowd.

Avoid any place which has a reputation for violence or unruly behaviour.

When faced with a dangerous situation remember one cardinal rule—DO NOT PANIC.

Panic

When faced with a sudden violent situation it is easy to panic. Should this happen the woman will be at a complete disadvantage because the logical thought process of her mind would be thrown into total confusion and, as a result of her anxiety, her bodily energy would be wasted in futile attempts to dislodge her aggressor by using up all her strength without resorting to the planned application of her resources. The weaker of the two must at all times rely upon presence of mind and positive action.

Variations

Obviously some attacks will not take place precisely as described in this book. An encyclopaedia would be required to cover all the possible variations which could occur. However, the specific situations described cover a very wide range of types of attack and the broad principles described remain valid across most of the possible variations. This book describes a number of types of attack and the simplest and most effective methods of dealing with them. The direct simplicity of the defences described lends itself to application in most of the variations likely to be encountered.

Darkness

It is difficult enough to face an aggressor in broad daylight when, in spite of the unpleasantness of the situation, you are still in full visual contact with all things around you. Should you be attacked during the hours of darkness, do try to remember that all things are exactly as they would be in daylight. The inability to see does not alter the fact that the situation is upon you but, as you cannot relate visually to the things around you, your imagination can run riot. Because a clear and concise picture is not being fed to the brain you must clear your mind and remember that the man is still just a man although shrouded by darkness and you still have the same powers of thought and physical reactions as you would have in perfect daylight. As in all other circumstances find the nearest available weak spot and strike without prejudice.

The main male points of weakness, especially selected for easy assailability by a female using hands, legs or weapons described in this book.

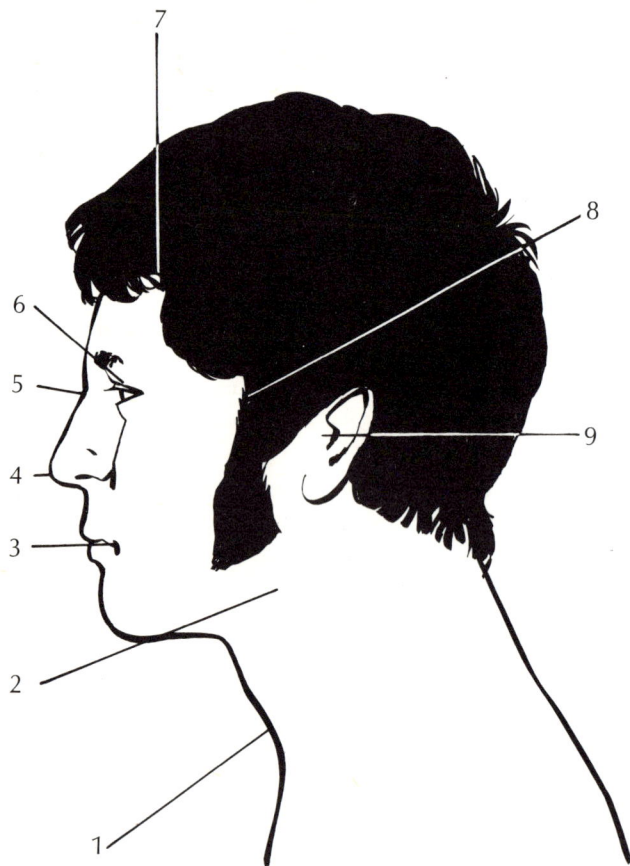

1 Adam's apple (punch or squeeze)
2 Corner of jaw (press inside and upwards)
3 Side of upper lip (twist)
4 Tip of nose (push upwards with heel of hand)
5 Bridge of nose (hit with hard object)
6 Pressure above eyeball, under bone (thumbs)
7 Front hairline (pull forwards)
8 Hair around temple (twist to rear)
9 Ear (striking area)

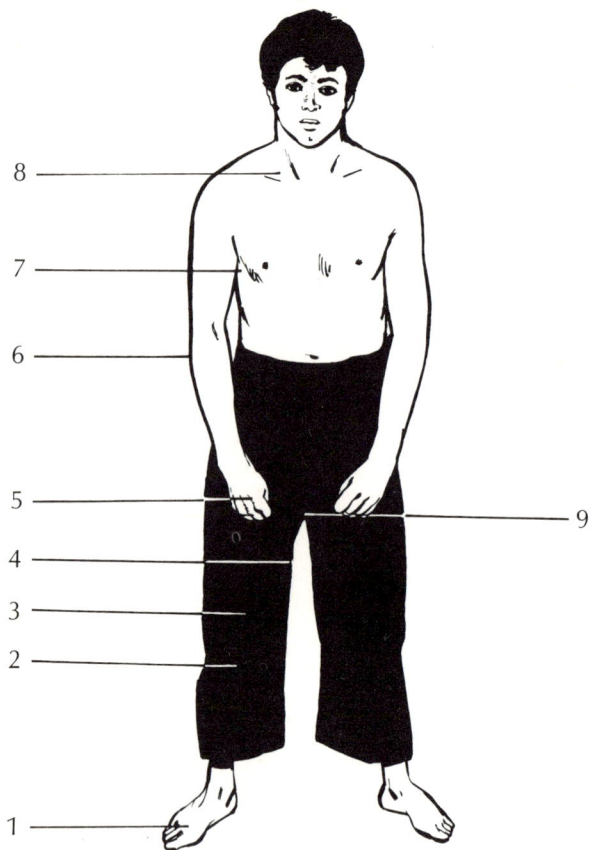

1 Bones just above toes (stamp or crush)
2 Shin (forward kick or scrape—area very sensitive to pain)
3 Kneecap (downward strike)
4 Inside leg, sensitive skin (pinch)
5 Bony upper hand (striking area)
6 Bone on elbow (striking area)
7 Soft skin underneath the arm (pinching)
8 Inside of collar bone (pressure point—press downwards)
9 Genital area (generally vulnerable)

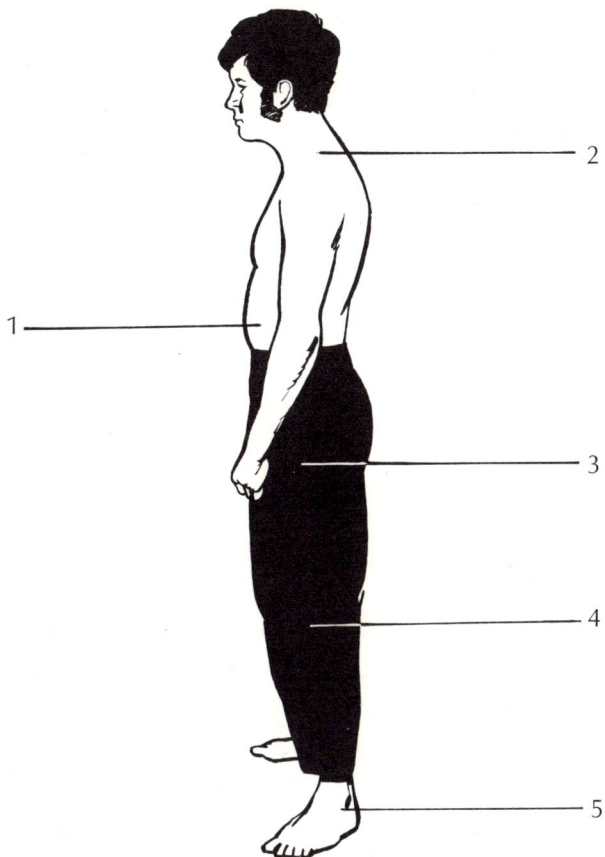

1 Lowest floating rib (striking or pushing)
2 Soft skin at side of neck (pinch or twist)
3 Wrist bone (striking)
4 Side of kneecap (direct kick)
5 Ankle bone (kick or grind)

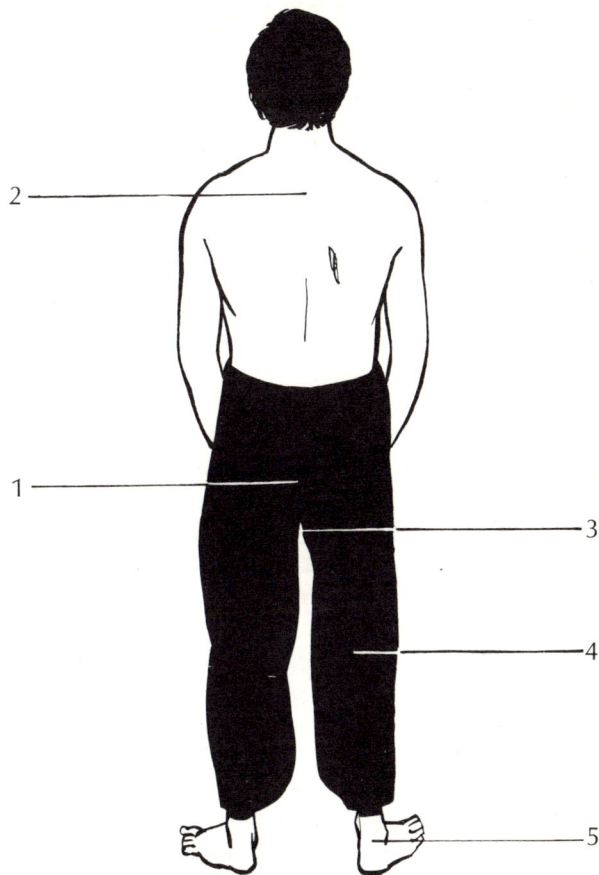

1 Tailbone (striking area)
2 Upper spine (striking area)
3 General genital area from underneath
4 Back of knee (push to throw off balance)
5 Achilles tendon (striking with side of shoe)

Example 1

You are attending a public function with many people present. The man becomes a nuisance but is unlikely, in company, to be potentially dangerous. Drastic methods are therefore not necessary—it is sufficient to demonstrate your knowledge and imply that any further amorous attempts will meet with immediate reprisals resulting in his public humiliation. It is most unlikely that any man will risk being laughed at in public.

Close the distance between you. Make certain that your outward manner appears to be completely non-aggressive.

Using the thumb and forefinger of your more available hand pinch the skin on the inside of his leg, halfway between the knee and groin. Remember to pinch the soft skin on the inside of the thigh.

Make certain that you withdraw your hand quickly. The man will react by lowering his hands to the injured spot, bending his body and jumping back.

Smile. Do appear normal and relaxed. Remember you want to prove a point and wish to avoid a scene.

Example 2

If you are attacked in an aggressive manner in which your hair is grabbed from the front;

Place both hands on the man's wrist. Step towards him.

Avoid the temptation to attack his exposed lower areas. You may well miss and if you do a struggle will develop. Should this happen, you are at a disadvantage because the man is stronger.

Bend your head and shoulder forward until you are able to slide under his arm, moving between his arm and his body.

His arm is now twisted behind his back. Don't force it up gradually, jerk it up quickly using both your hands. His face is now exposed to an attack from your knee or foot, if you have not already floored him.

Example 3

Someone places his hand roughly on your shoulder from the rear.

Step back so that your bodies are side by side.

This will only work if you step back to his side and are standing close to the aggressor. Any attempt to keep a respectful distance will result in a struggle where again the advantage is his.

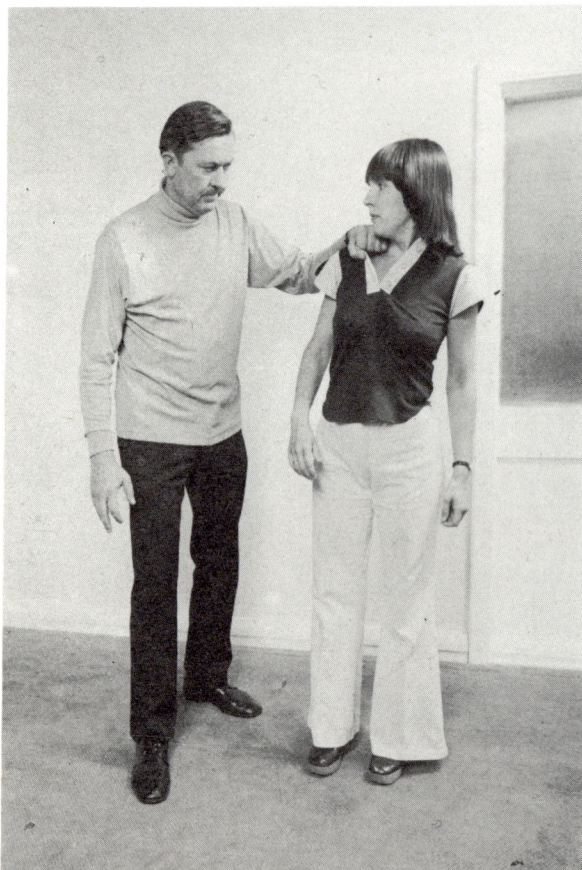

Move your arm nearest to him in a high arc to avoid the man's head and bring it up trapping his arm above the elbow.

Support it with your other hand.

At this point the amount of pressure you apply is entirely up to you. You can;
a) **Press with all your strength in a jerking movement and dislocate his arm.**
b) **Press hard enough to hold him steady while you bring your knee up and deliver a downward kick to his lower abdomen.**
c) **Using your supporting arm bring your open palm downwards and very hard onto the tip of his nose.**
d) **Bring him down by continuing the pressure backwards.**

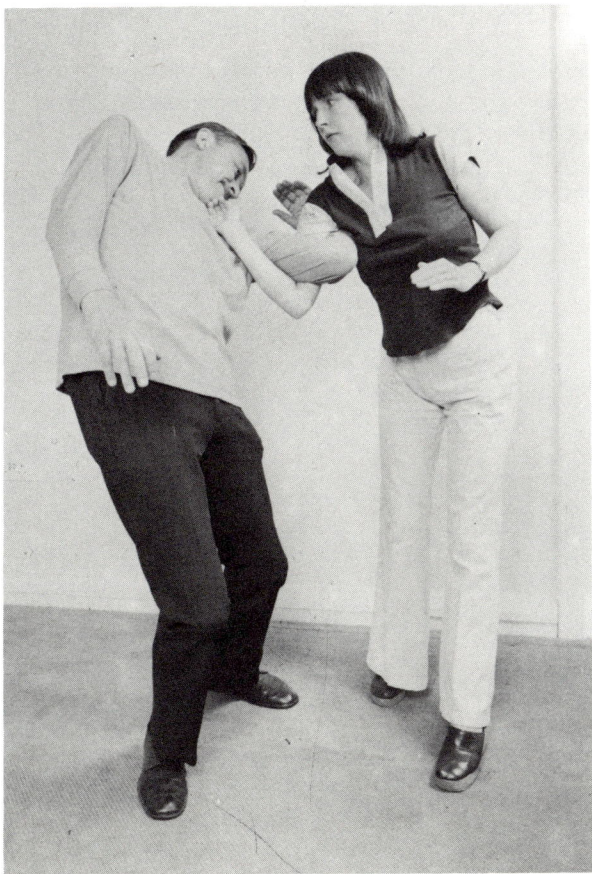

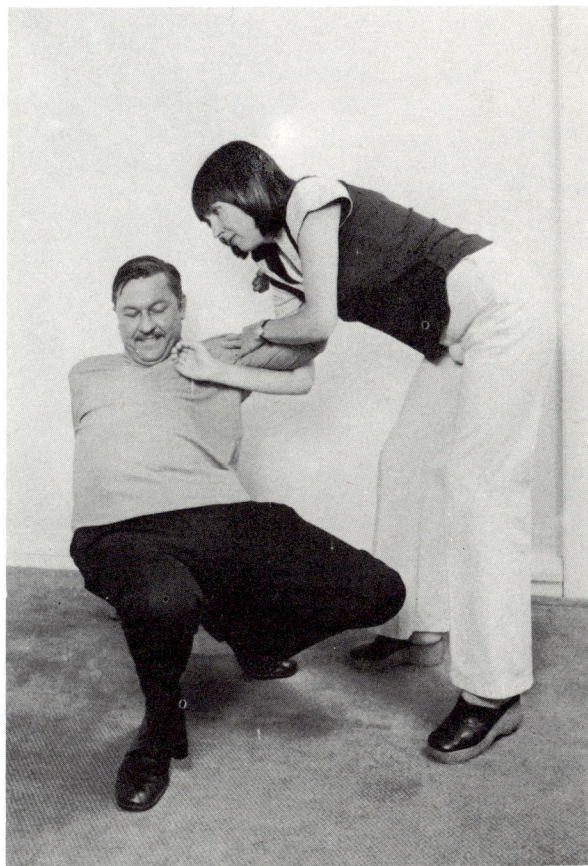

Example 4

A man has decided to caress you amorously and has placed his hand on your breast. You must determine the seriousness of this situation before acting. If you decide it is potentially dangerous;

Put both hands on his shoulders or behind his head. Move forward as if to embrace him and make bodily contact.

As you do this, place your weight on one leg and bring your knee to his genital area at the same time pushing the palm of your hand into his mouth or nose.

Remember, you must put your hands on him or arms round him to maintain your balance. To avoid suspicion and to camouflage your movements, a smile on your face helps a lot.

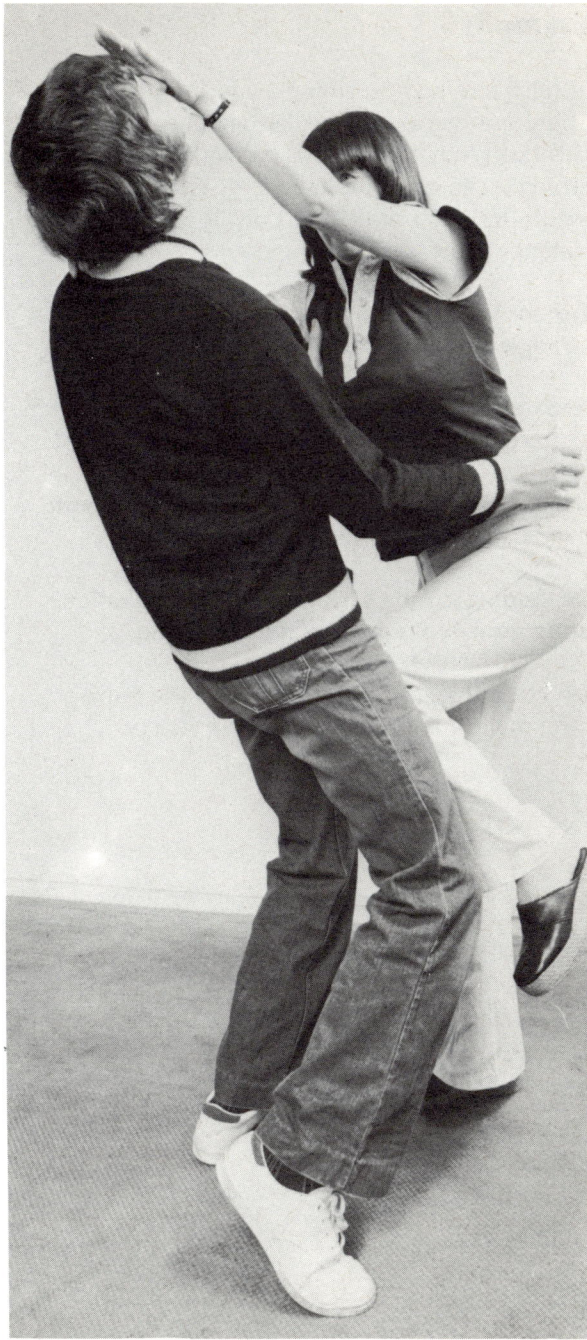

Example 5

A man attempts to strangle you from behind. There are many spectacular defences against this but remember time is precious, an effective strangle can be completed in 4 seconds, the victim losing control after only 1½ seconds. Your defence must work first time.

Do not try to peel off his hands. He cannot strangle you from a distance.

Arch your body outwards and bring your rear as hard as you can into his lower abdomen.

Bend down and grab one of his legs with both hands and jerk it upwards.

Depending on the seriousness of the situation, bring your foot down as in the picture.

Do not panic, this only cuts down the narrow time margin and wastes precious energy.

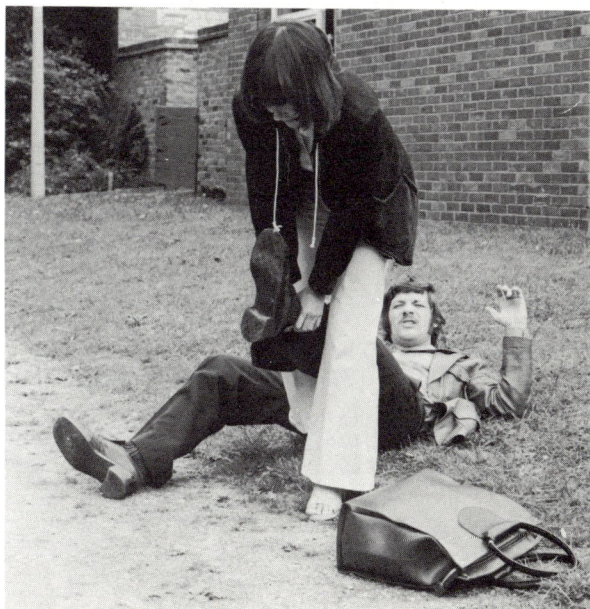

Example 6

A man attempts to strangle you from the front. Again, you must be aware of the brief time in which to act and of the great danger of the situation. Do not try to pull his hands off or punch him. He will not feel a thing.

This will only work at close quarters so do remember to thrust your body at him.

Grab his ears, or hair close to the temple as near to the skin as possible, between your thumb and forefinger.

Don't pull—pushing in, rotate backwards in a circular movement with both hands simultaneously. This will cause him to pull back his head in considerable pain. Taking advantage of this pain thrust your knee into his genitals.

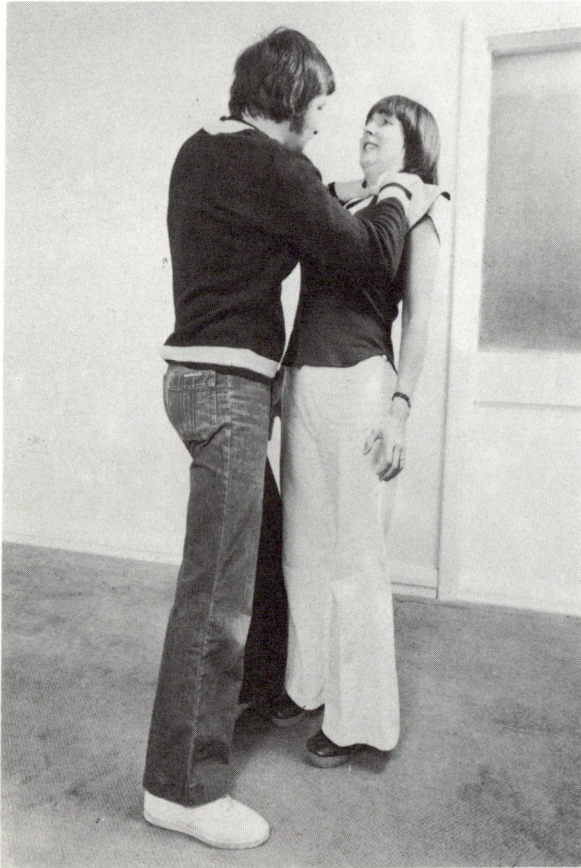

Example 7

This is a variation on the previous defence against a front strangle. Again, remember the limited time factor. It must work first time.

Slide your thumbs into the corners of his mouth. Pull outwards and backwards. The pain that this will inevitably cause him will again give you the opportunity of thrusting your knee into his genitals.

Example 8

You are held in an overarm bear hug from the front. This time you do not have to close the distance between you and your assailant—you are close enough.

Push the top of your head towards his mouth and nose. Pinch the inside of his thigh as in *example 1* **or attack his very vulnerable lower parts.**

If you are completely pinned, then slide your mouth towards his lips and bite them hard.

Example 9

Now you are held in an underarm front bear hug. Both your attacker's hands are committed but you have your hands and legs free.

You may attack the facial areas as in *examples 6 and 7* or;

Grab hold of one eyebrow. Grab hold of the soft skin under his jaw. Like turning a driving wheel, pull down with your right hand and up with your left. Bring your knee up.

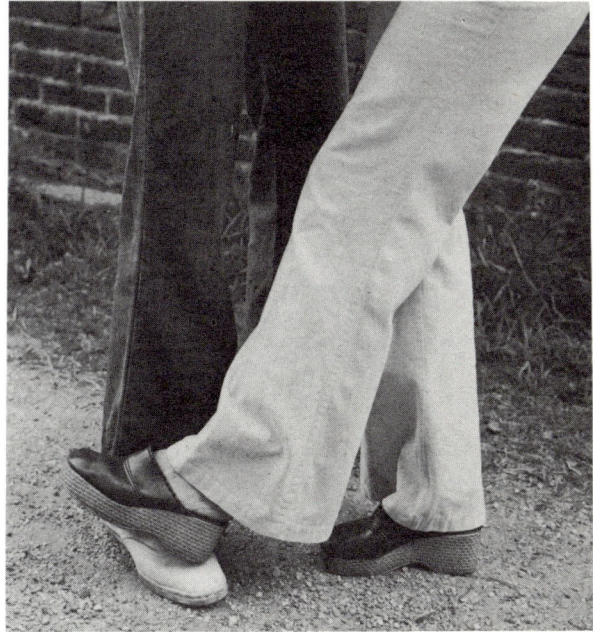

Bring your heel down onto his toes. It is possible if you twist your heel on impact to damage the bones of his foot.

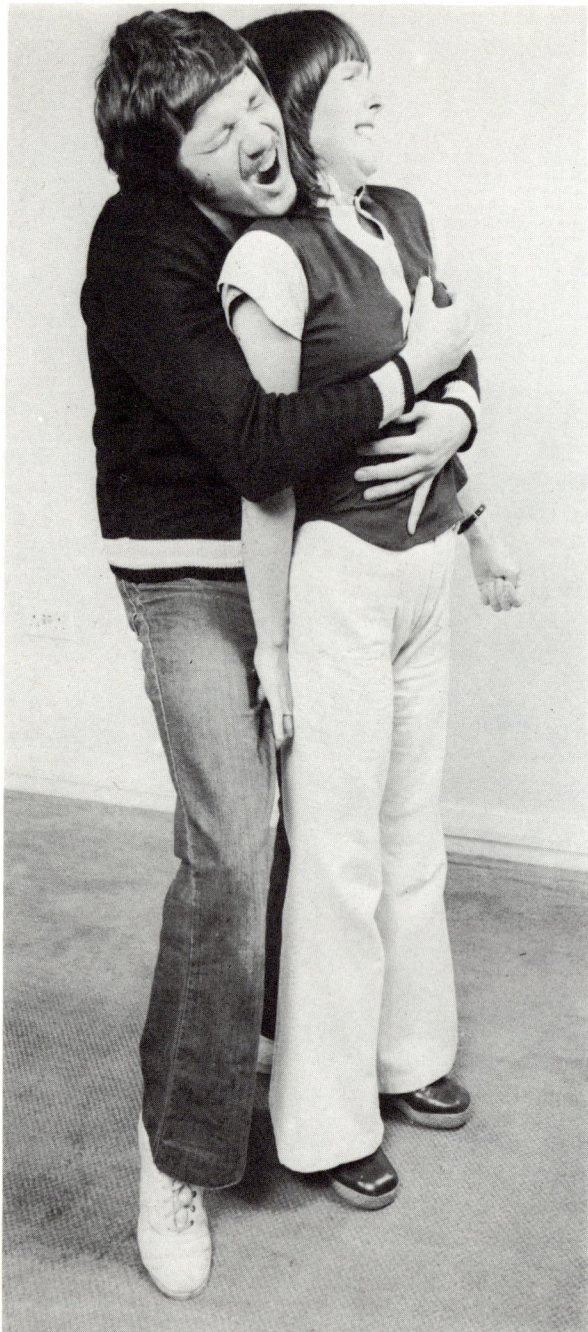

Example 10

An attacker has you in an overarm bear hug from behind so your arm movements are restricted.

Bring the back of your head sharply to his face. Pinch the insides of his thighs with both hands or, claw upwards at his genital area. You may alternatively use the technique in *example 5.*

Example 11

In an underarm bear hug from the rear you may use the technique for an overarm bear hug, *example 10,* but as you now have the use of your arms you may apply the following;

Lean against him so that your head is by the side of his. Slide your fingers under his lips and pull, simultaneously kicking backwards with your heel. Do remember that in any bear hug it is quite useless to tug to remove the grip with force.

Example 12

Your car stops at traffic lights or a road junction. An intruder forces his way in. Do not try to force him out. Let him push his way in. Switch off the car engine.

Sitting beside you he will be half-turned towards you; he cannot do much facing the front of the car. Be obliging—turn towards him.

Form the fingers of your right hand into a claw and push upwards into his face, catching the tip of his nose. Slide over as if getting on top of him.

While doing this slide your right knee over and bring your full weight on it onto his genitals. Bring your right elbow to his face. Get out quickly and get assistance.

Example 13

If a man makes a nuisance of himself while sitting beside you on public transport or on a park bench, you may respond as in *example 12,* or merely sharply kick his nearest ankle, or;

Put your arm round his neck and butt his face sharply with your head. Bring your free arm to his genitals and lean heavily on it. Having inflicted the pain, release yourself and get help.

Example 14

A man confronts you in a doorway or a place where your space may be somewhat limited. Take advantage of your close proximity to your assailant, moving in towards him.

Put your arms around his neck and grab his hair close to the skin above the neckline. Turn your hands inwards and then pull downwards. This will cause him to bend forward into a perfect position for an attack to the groin with your knee.

If you think the position warrants it, using the driving wheel technique, twist his head to the left thus getting him sufficiently off-balance to attack the toes of his right foot with your right heel.

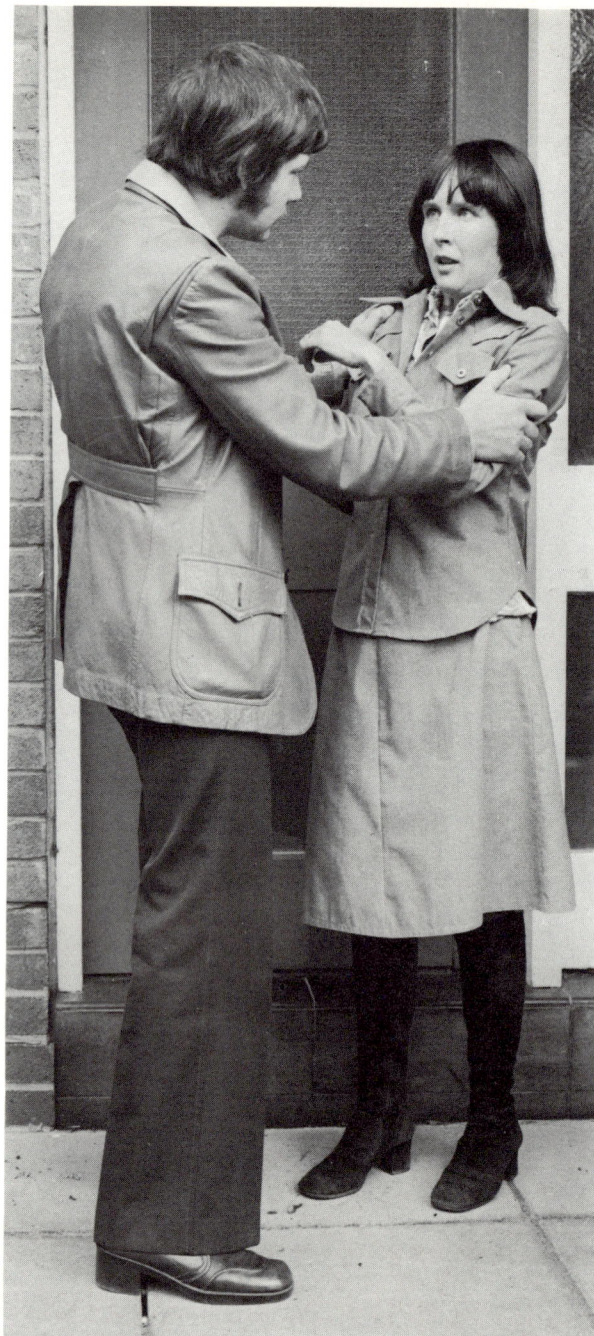

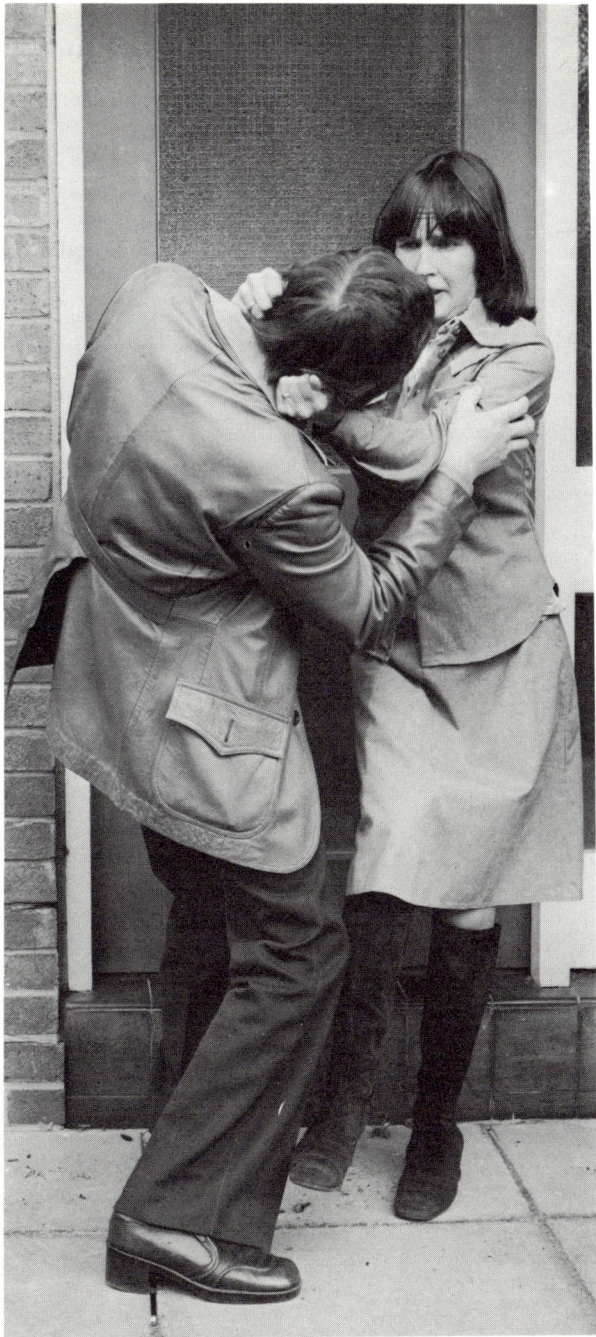

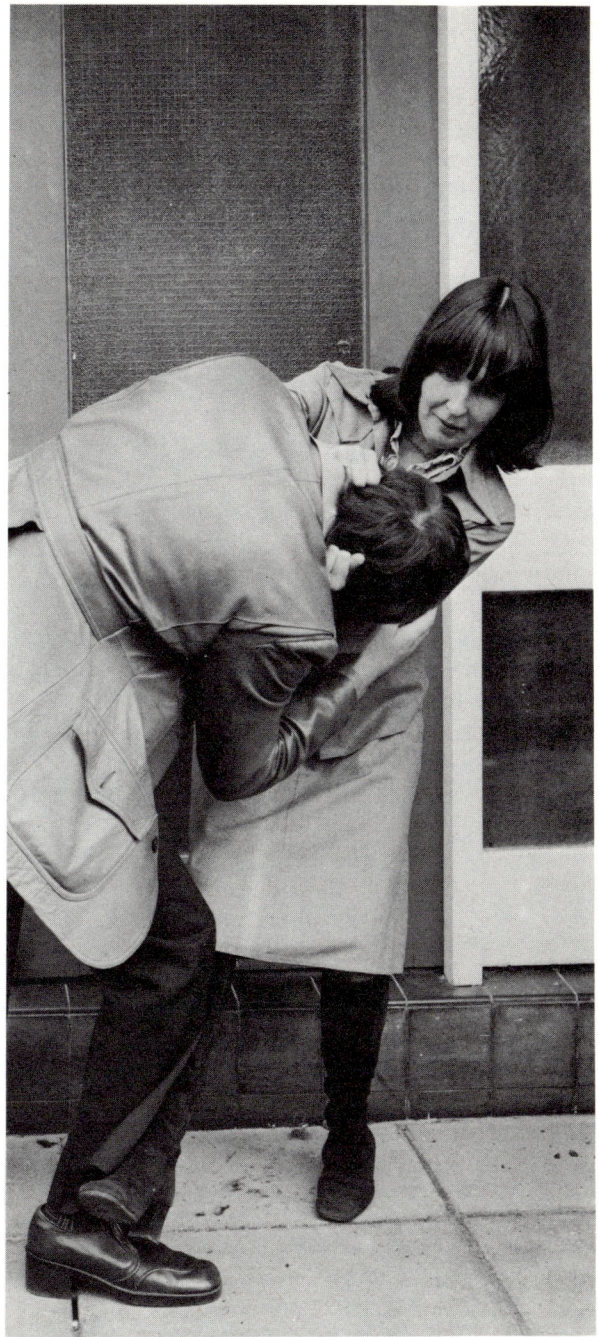

Example 15

If you are assaulted while ascending or descending a flight of stairs do try to reach level ground if at all possible. If you are wearing high-heeled shoes, kick them off. You will be at a distinct disadvantage even if you are only slightly off balance.

Move in and make decisive attacks to his face and eyes or mouth. As soon as you have inflicted pain upon him break contact and run. The picture illustrates a typical attack; Twisting of left ear to cause pain and affect balance. Simultaneous attack to soft parts of the face with your left elbow—this technique works best in a double movement. Bring the elbow upwards to attack your opponent's face. Should contact not be made, bring the elbow downwards thus giving yourself a second chance of hitting the target. Your balance is maintained by your right hand—this leaves your left leg free to attack any vulnerable part.

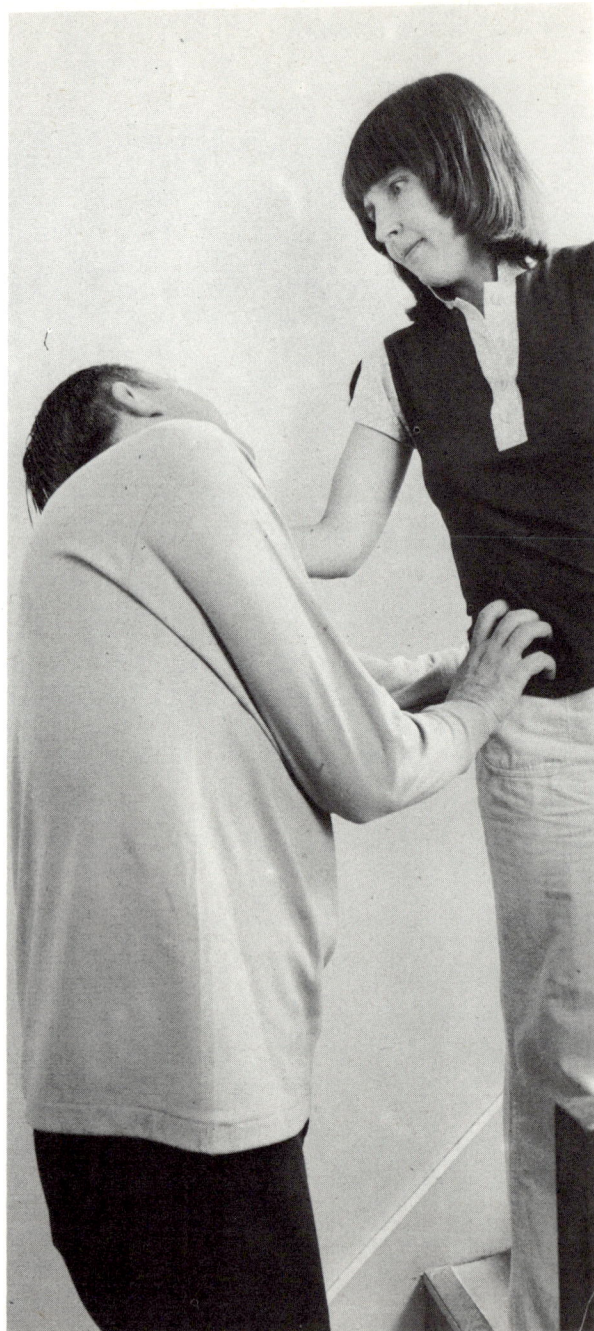

Example 16

A man has approached you in an obviously aggressive manner. You mustn't be concerned for his feelings now.

Grab one of his hands with both yours with the palms of your hands on the back of his and your thumbs across his wrist.

Turn his palm upwards. Roll the palm outwards towards his hip. Continued use of this movement will force the man to the ground with no difficulty.

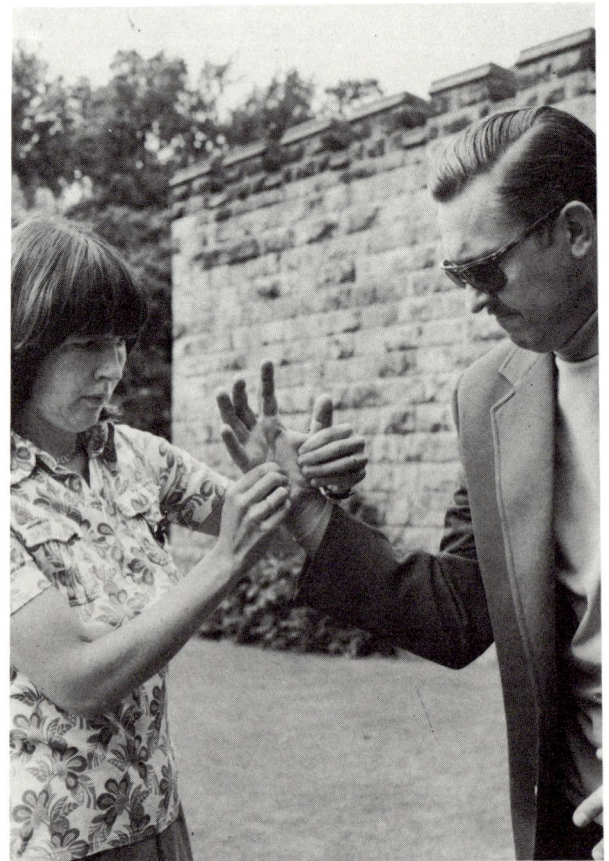

At this point no actual pain has been inflicted as can be seen by the bemused look on the attacker's face. However, a look at his left leg indicates that he is already totally off balance.

As an alternative method, when the aggressor is sufficiently off balance kick any vulnerable area within the middle regions of his body. Kick only at a definite vulnerable target.

Example 17

You are walking down a lonely lane. You slip and land on your back. At this moment a lurking male emerges from behind a bush and jumps on top of you. Assuming your arms are free;

Slide the palm of your hand edge upwards and strike a glancing blow at the tip of his nose.

Grab his mouth with your hand and twist it round (either one or both lips). This must be a firm decisive movement, pressing the grabbed skin together and inwards and at the same time twisting sharply. This will cause your assailant to pull back and enable you to make a swift getaway.

Example 18

If a man has you on the ground with both your arms pinned you must not struggle. As long as you are held in this way little else can happen. Should he require his hand elsewhere he will have to free one of your arms. Once this happens use the technique described in *example 17.*

Example 19

You have been grabbed from behind and thrown to the ground.

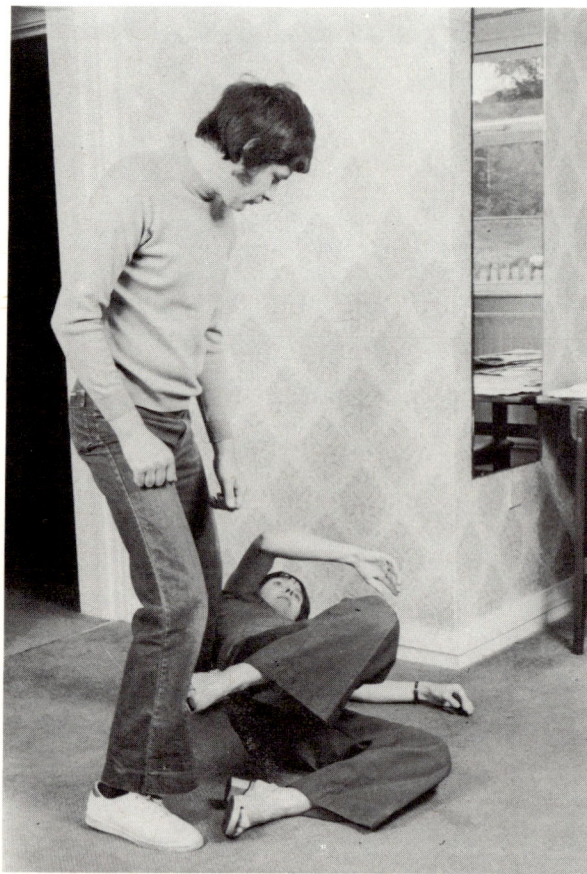

If your attacker attempts to kick you, trip him either with a foot behind his knee and one in front of his shin which will bring him forward.

If he wants to jump on top of you let him, then use one of the methods of defence previously described in *examples 17* and *18*. Avoid the danger of his attacking you while you are getting up; if you are off balance and a struggle develops you will get hurt.

Or with a foot behind his heel and in front of his knee which will bring him backwards.

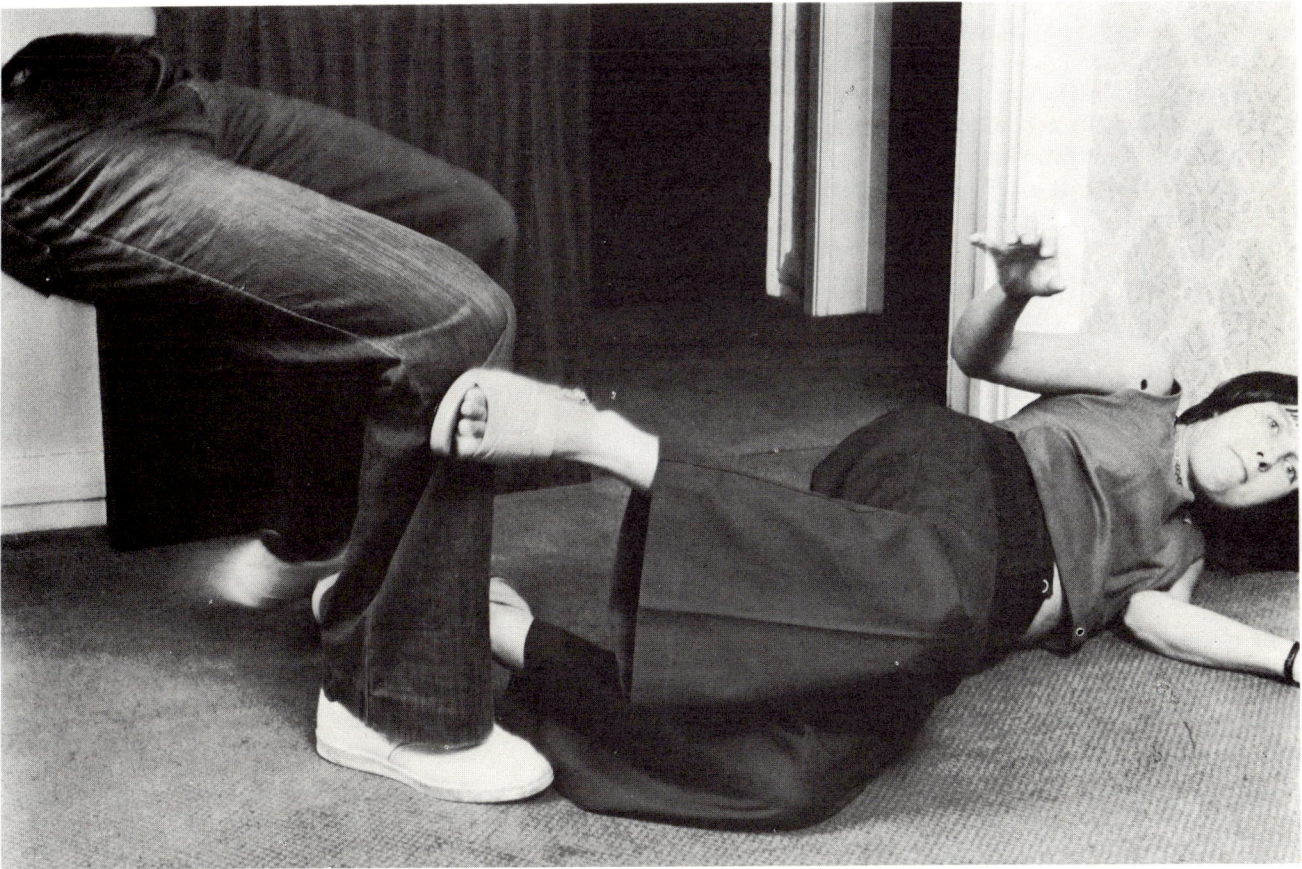

Example 20

A man grabs you from the rear and your arms are pinned down. Another man takes hold of your skirt from the front. You have two attackers to deal with—do not struggle wildly in order to dislodge them both at once. You must deal with them one at a time.

For a second, ignore the man in front and deal with the one behind you as you would in *example 10* **(head back and double pinch to thighs or genitals) to save time as you have a second opponent.**

Having removed the menace from behind you can now concentrate on the man in front. Grab the skin round his throat and pull down. Bring your knee up to his genital area or use any alternative method previously described.

N.B. A girl's natural reaction would be to tackle the man in front. If she attempts to fight off her frontal adversary while firmly held from the rear, the results will be an uneven struggle where a girl's strength is pitted against that of two men. This would obviously prove disastrous in a short space of time. Remember therefore to dispose of the man to your *rear* first as only then can you give the man in *front* your undivided attention.

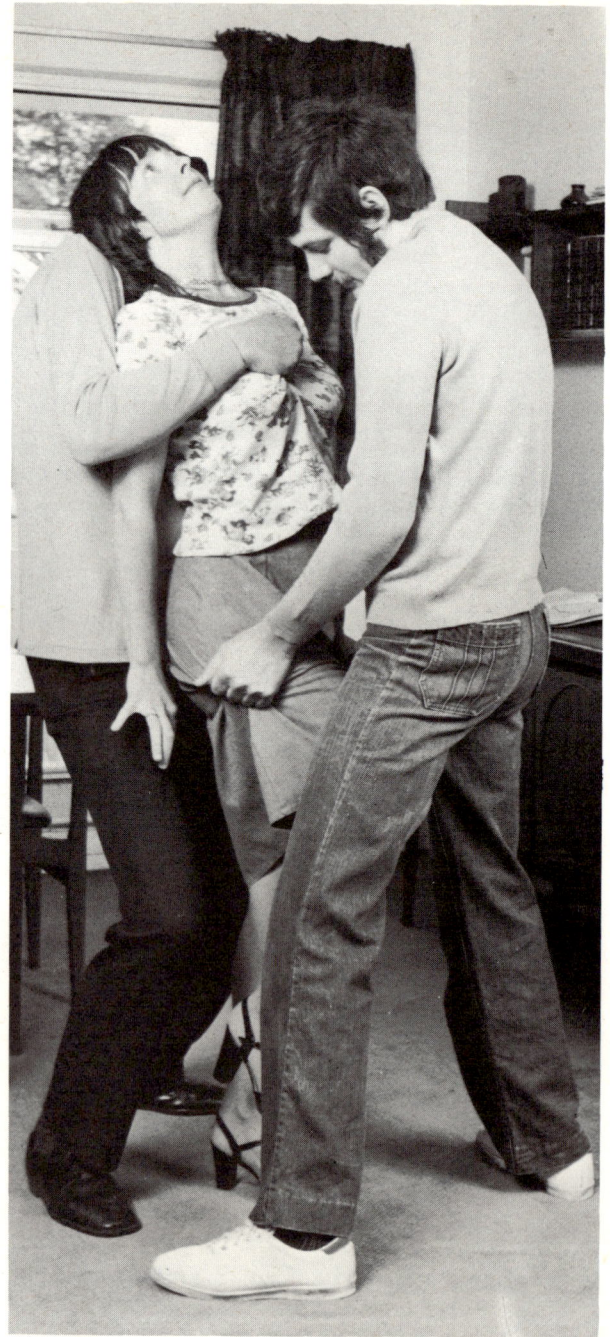

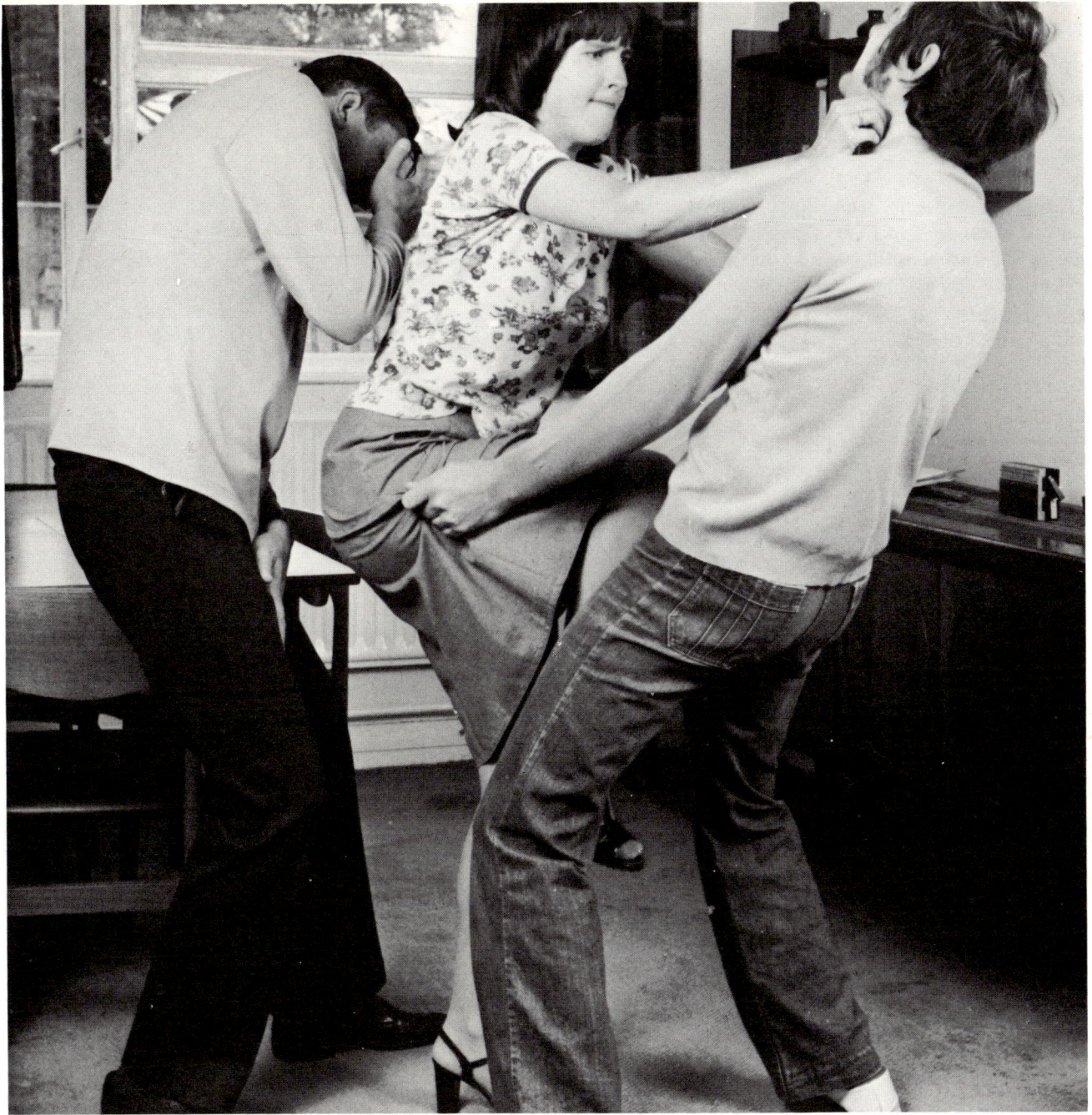

Example 21

You are sitting on a couch. A man sitting next to you chooses to make unmistakably unpleasant advances. You wish to get free swiftly and permanently.

Let him put his arms around you. Turn towards him. While doing this move one hand towards the gentle and sensitive skin on the inside of his leg and the other hand upwards towards his face.

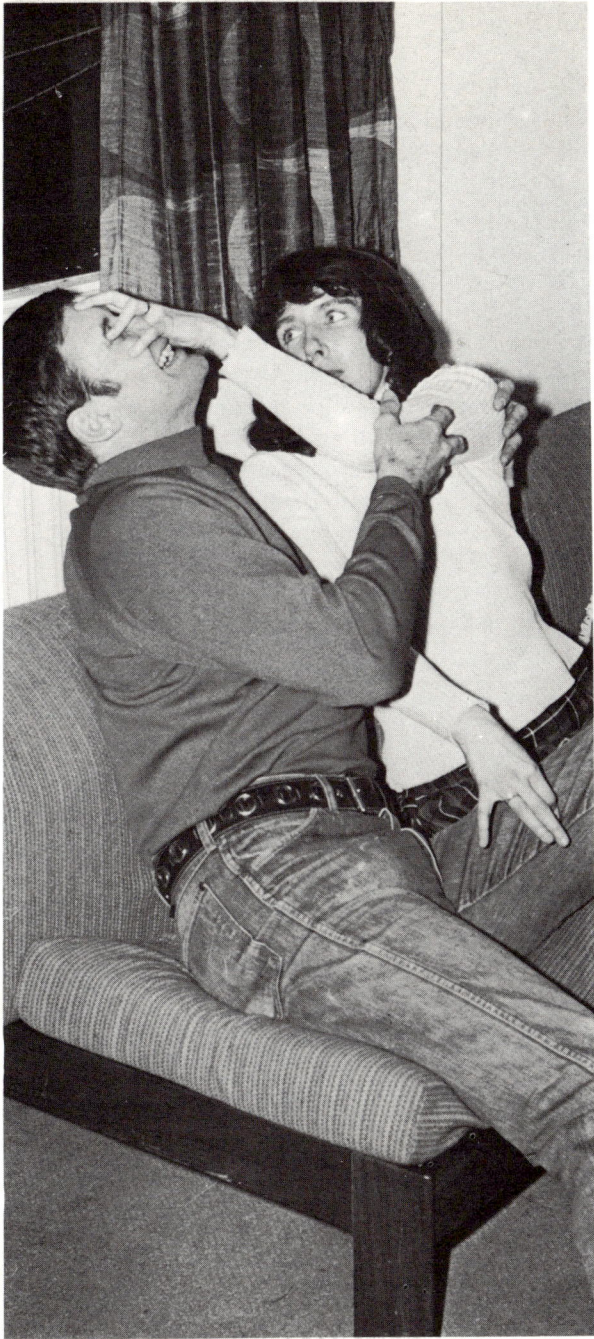

Simultaneously pinch his leg, drive the palm of your hand to the tip of his nose and, if necessary, attack the eyes with your fingertips. Move away as swiftly as possible.

Example 22

You are in a nasty position. Follow-up photographs are not provided because at this stage you may use your imagination and find your own solutions from the descriptions given below. This is done to encourage you to think for yourself as total reliance upon a series of given situations is not practical.

You are in a vicious grip but you have one free arm. Your attacker has committed all his limbs. You can bite or attack his eyes or throat or, relax completely and go limp in his arms pressing slightly towards him. Form a circle by joining the tips of your thumb and forefinger. Extend your remaining fingers upwards. Hook the circle round his nose and press upwards and inwards. The weakest hand has more power than the bridge of the nose.

Example 23

You are at a bus stop with no people present except yourself and the attacker. There is no visible assistance so you must act quickly to gain control of your attacker and the situation. When your assailant commits himself and you realise that quick physical action is the only possible answer, manoeuvre yourself into a position from which you can strike with the greatest advantage.

Bring the edge of your left foot sharply across the line of his toes. Slightly cupping your hand, draw it sharply upwards so that the knuckles jerk violently against his nostrils. Turn and walk away quickly. Do not run.

If you happen to have an umbrella, swing it sharply between his legs or stab downwards upon his toe. Do not attempt to hit him on his head as this will most likely be stopped and if it is not, it will not cause sufficient discomfort to enable you to check your opponent with your first technique.

Example 24

If you are at a bus stop with people present a milder form of defence is adequate. The psychological effect of ridicule from onlookers when trying to hide the pain from a sharp kick is enough to remove any man's unwanted attentions.

Maintain your balance by holding the lapel of his jacket and bring your foot heavily onto his foot.

A kick to the shin which may or may not be followed by a sharp stab to the toe is again designed to cause sufficient pain and embarrassment to dissuade the aggressor from any further advances.

Example 25

If you are assaulted while alone in an underground station you must deal firmly with your opponent in order to get away. If there is more than one, then your defence must be more conclusive.

A bunch of keys pushed firmly into your opponent's nostrils will give you ample time to get away from him.

If there are people around grab your opponent's collar and with your left arm push your knuckles under his Adam's apple. Straighten your arm pushing his head backwards. Grab him by the belt with your right arm and pull it towards you. This will tilt him backwards into a position from which he will be only too pleased to escape in order to avoid embarrassment.

N.B. Unless your knuckles are firmly just under his Adam's apple this technique will rely on strength and should be avoided.

Example 26

A man makes an obvious nuisance of himself in an underground train. Discourage him verbally, then change your seat, but if this does not work then dissuade him by attacking some Atemi points.

Grab the soft skin behind the jawline between the thumb and forefinger. Press firmly together. You can;

a) **rotate your hands away from you to move him backwards thus exposing him to a follow-up attack;**

b) **or rotate your hands backwards and to the side exposing his face to a sharp attack to the nose.**

Alternative methods of disposing of an underground nuisance are as follows:

Pinch both sides of his neck, stamp on his toe immediately, and change your seat.
If he is being thoroughly obnoxious—guiding your elbow with your opposite hand, ram it into his throat or face.

If a man presses himself to you in an indecent manner in a crowded underground train do not shout or make a scene—a sharp pinch to the sensitive skin on the inside of his thigh will deter him and to the public eye will pass quite unnoticed.

Example 27

You are in a train compartment with an aggressor. Remember he may not be a rapist but a mere opportunist. Remember too, however, that you must gain control of him in order to give yourself time to raise the alarm.

You have decided to kick your assailant's ankle. You stand up placing one arm upon his shoulder—this enables you to stand steady against the motion of the train, gives you the correct distance for an accurate kick and leaves him slightly puzzled giving you time to execute your manoeuvre. Deliver a sharp kick to the ankle.

Should this be insufficient grab his hair above the ear with both hands pushing downwards. Ram your forehead hard into his face. This technique, although unpleasant, is very effective and its use is recommended when you are alone.

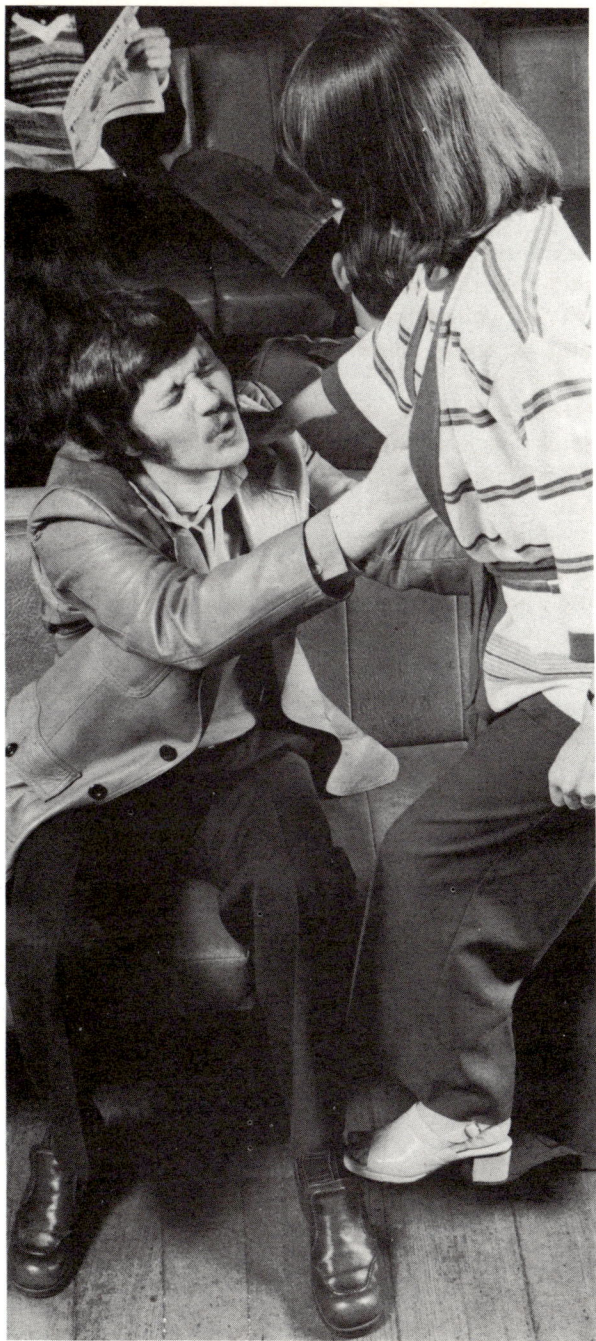

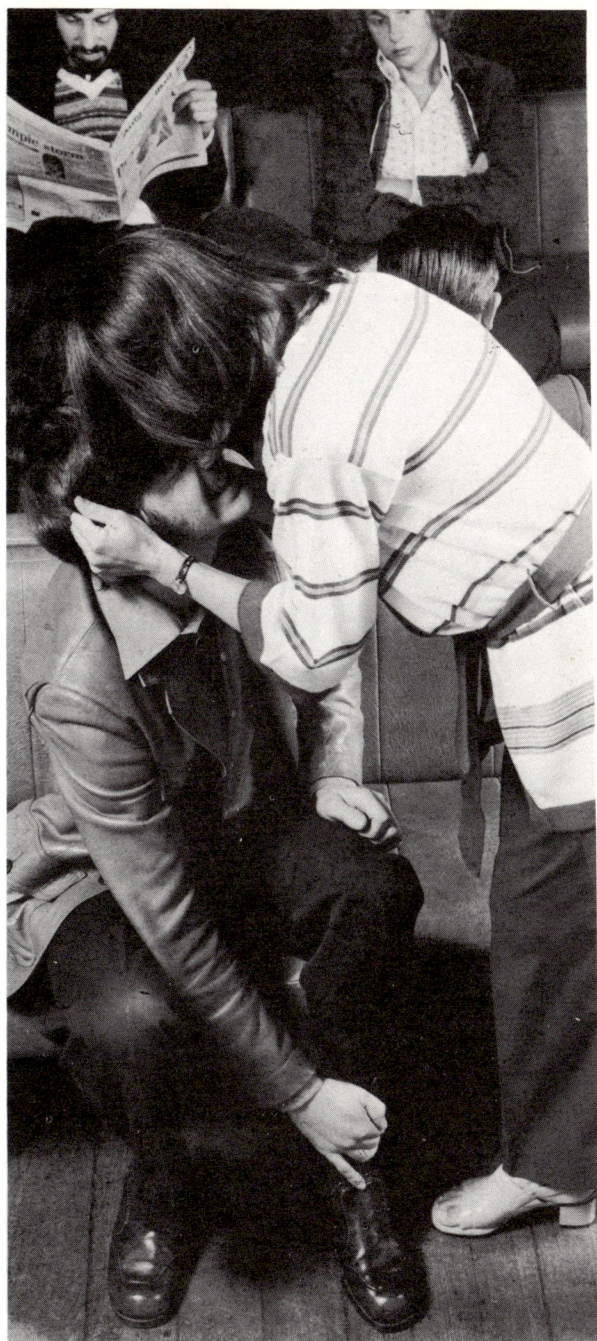

Example 28

If you are pestered in a street during the day, with people around, you must hurt the man sufficiently to stop his pursuit thus gaining time to mix with people and get out of the way.

Administer two sharp pinches, one to the soft skin of his neck, the other under his breast, leaving your opponent unmistakably cringing and attracting attention to himself, not to you.

N.B. The idea that attackers can be distracted by the woman screaming often backfires. When alone, screaming can provoke an attack out of fear. When amongst people, the aggressor will disappear into a doorway or mingle with the crowd while the eyes of the passers-by are all focused upon you, screaming to no effect.

Example 29

If possible avoid being in an unlit street at night, but if you are alone and you are attacked your action must be conclusive as there may be no one to come to your assistance.

Screw the skin on the neck of your attacker with one hand. Move your other hand into his face so that the soft skin between your thumb and forefinger is under his nose—press and push upwards. This leaves his lower area completely exposed should you decide to follow up, otherwise break away and disappear into the shadows.

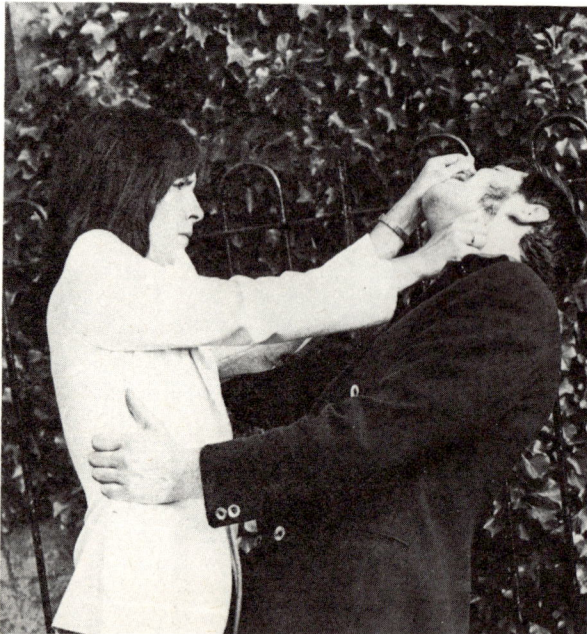

Example 30

You find yourself at a rowdy party and, either through ignorance or gullibility, have been manoeuvred to a secluded part of the house. The man makes positive physical advances towards you leaving you in no doubt as to his intentions. If you are unable merely to leave, try a more subtle approach first. If this fails;

Grab hold of his belt with both hands. Jerk it violently upwards. As a result of this action the seam of his trousers will come into very violent contact with his genitals. The time which it would take to resume his dignity should be sufficient to allow you to slip away. Alternatively, grab hold of his pubic hair and jerk violently upwards. The result is equally unpleasant. Under these circumstances avoid going for his genitals as a slight miscalculation of touch may give him totally the wrong idea.

If the above-mentioned manoeuvre is difficult and his advances are very persistent, strike the area between his upper lip and nose and press with your knuckles against his nostrils towards the rear. This should hurt him and put him in a position of imbalance which will allow you to bring your knee into action should it be necessary, which is doubtful. Again you have gained sufficient time to leave the scene.

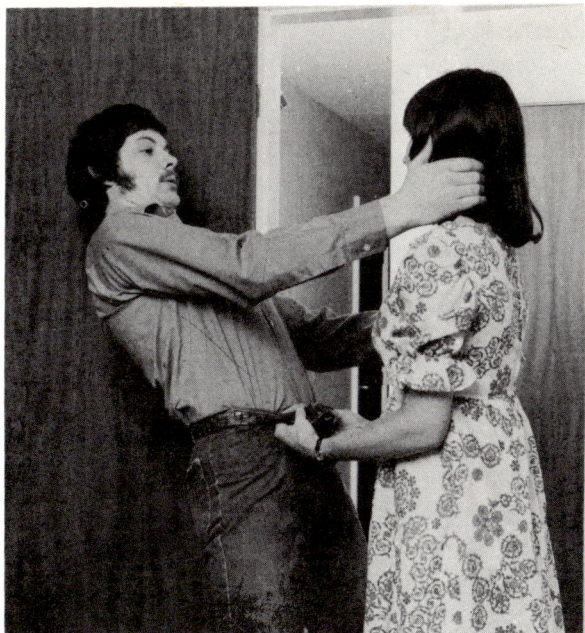

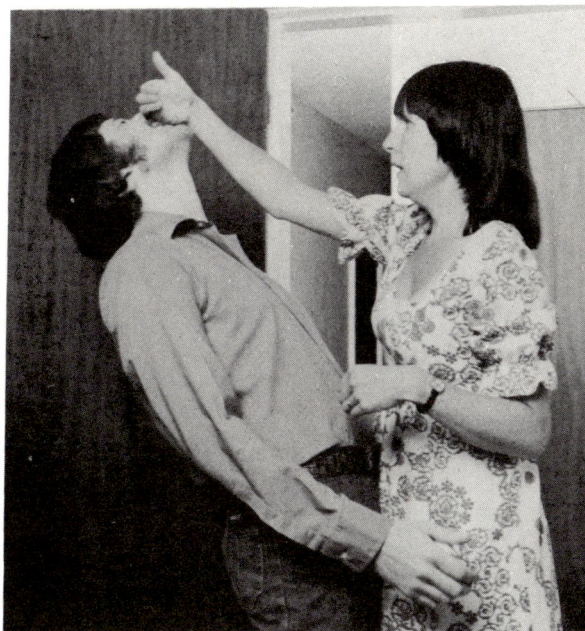

Example 31

You are enjoying a drink in a bar. All is quiet. The barman has left his post and assistance is not available. You do not want to waste your drink by spilling it over the man who is paying you unwanted attentions. You wish to put him out of action for only a short period of time.

Grab a fistful of hair just above his temple. Rotate your wrists forwards or backwards to cause pain. Place your fingers firmly under his Adam's apple and jab upwards sharply.

While your opponent is spluttering you should have all the time you need to finish your drink in peace.

Example 32

If you are assaulted in a noisy crowded bar you must assess the situation. You must cause sufficient discomfort to cool him off or to get away yourself by causing a nose bleed or by inflicting a hand pinch to his leg or underarm.

As well as the above you may decide to kick him sharply on the ankle and walk away, or slide your arm under his jacket and pinch as hard as you can with fingers and thumb under his breast.

In both cases it will cause sufficient pain to make him cringe and attract attention to himself. At this point he will have to grin and bear it as the alternatives are attacking a woman openly in a crowded place or shattering his pride by showing that physical pain was caused by a mere female.

Example 33

If you are accosted outside a bar you must make a firm, positive move in order to gain time to leave.

Having once decided upon the action when the assault becomes positive please remember that the contact between the heel of your hand and his nose must be sufficiently vigorous to prove your point the first time. A half-hearted attempt will result in a struggle.

Alternatively you may;

a) Bring the side of your foot sharply onto his toes.

b) Follow through with a grinding movement, rotating your toes inwards.

c) As he bends forward, slip your left arm under his chin and grab his lapel. This places the bony part of your lower arm to his Adam's apple. Using your free hand push his head firmly onto your arm causing a spasm of spluttering.

You should now be able to move away in peace, but please remember that assistance would be available if you returned into the bar or hotel.

Example 34

If a man makes a nuisance of himself in a cinema, try to dissuade him verbally or if possible move your place.

If his arm goes around your shoulders grab the hair above his temple and give it a good sharp tug. If he is wearing a tie give one of the ends a hard pull so that it will start to choke him. If he puts his hand on your knee ask in a loud, clear voice 'Can I help you?'

If he persists, stick a sharp object—hairpin, pin, pencil, into the top of his hand.

Example 35

If you are annoyed at a public concert, verbal dissuasion should be sufficient. Under the circumstances attacking Atemi points of the face may not become necessary. Also, you might not want to disturb other people.

If a polite reprimand is unsuccessful grab the soft skin between the thumb and forefinger and twist sharply inwards or outwards.

Example 36

The following situations may arise when you go alone to the theatre, or at any public function where you may find yourself sitting in a row of seats with people in front and behind and with an amorous male pest by your side. Assume that your gentle hint has failed, your words have failed and you either cannot or do not choose to leave your seat.

Pinch and twist the skin either just below or just above the back of the knee.

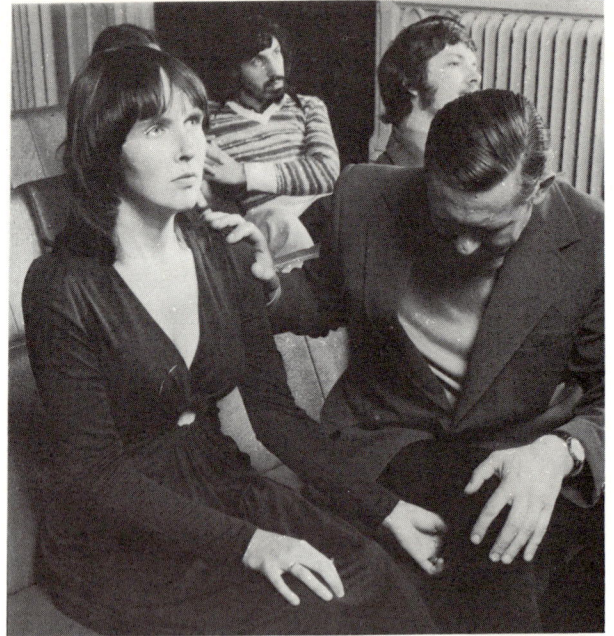

As his leg presses against yours, screw your ring just above his kneecap on the bone.

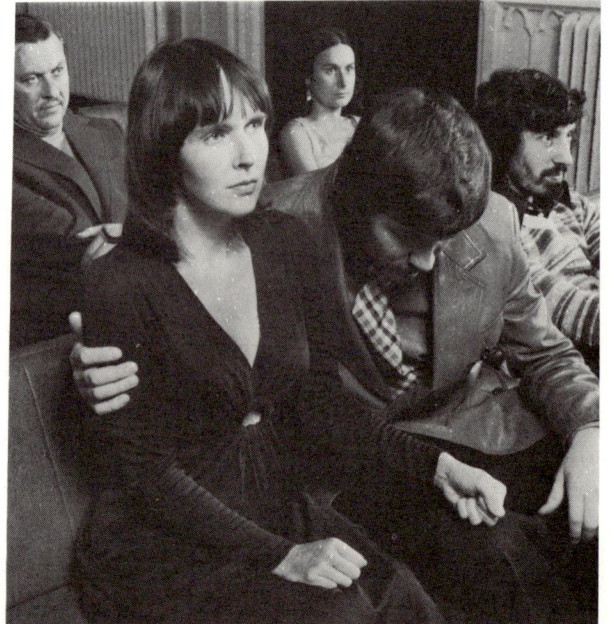

Should his attention be not so much amorous as clearly vulgar, push a pencil, pen or any sharp object at hand under the jaw bone. In this case you have placed your left arm across his body on his wrist to prevent his right arm coming up and interfering with your action.

In the case of similar aggression of a very vulgar nature, if you happen to have a cigarette in your hand which is lighted shove it between the buttons of his shirt, immediately giving it a sharp tap with the outstretched palm of your other hand to ensure that the treatment properly takes effect.

69

Example 37

You are at an afternoon fête or social occasion with people constantly around. Get away from any unwanted attention if at all possible.

'Accidentally' spill a cup of tea or coffee—this causes discomfort and embarrassment. Smile with feeling and look as if the whole act was accidental. If you really wish to rub it in, apologise.
If the degree of vulgarity is more pronounced you react accordingly by;
a) tipping the tea into his face or,
b) pouring it just above the belt down the inside of his trousers.

This does not hurt. However, a person with cream all over his face amongst people is highly unlikely to continue his amorous advances. While he is wiping his face you have ample time to slip away.

Example 38

If you are accosted in a lift remember you are in a confined space and there will also be a restricted time limit. If you can put up with a few moments' embarrassment let it pass, otherwise, act as follows.

Grabbing hold of his upper lip pull upwards. This momentarily exposes his lower areas as the pain is quite sharp.

Steadying yourself on his shoulder, deliver a kick to his genitals using the whole of your shin to avoid missing at a first attempt as a struggle in very confined quarters must be avoided.

Example 39

If you are in a confined space such as by a river or canal, or in an alleyway and are approached aggressively from front and rear, you cannot possibly evade the attack. You must allow the attackers to come to close quarters, relax and pick your move, and tackle one at a time. Do not struggle.

For a fraction of a second ignore the man behind you. Grab the man in front by his ear and pull him downwards. Simultaneously strike a glancing blow against his nose with the heel of your other hand. Bring your knee sharply up. Please remember that these techniques will work when he is within range. Let him come close enough to make your attack successful.

With your right hand, claw the face of the man behind or grab his hair. Bring your left shoulder up sharply to meet his face. With your left hand, pinch the soft skin inside his leg or if the man you first attacked shows signs of recovery unceremoniously administer a sharp squeeze to his genitals.

Example 40

You wish to enter a modern block of flats. A gang of hooligans is blocking your path. If possible find another way in or wait until they have dispersed. If necessary, use a policeman to escort you in, otherwise use the 'count three and move' principle—plan a positive attack to three of them and move right through. You must have planned your moves and picked your targets beforehand. The movements must be accurate, positive and quick.

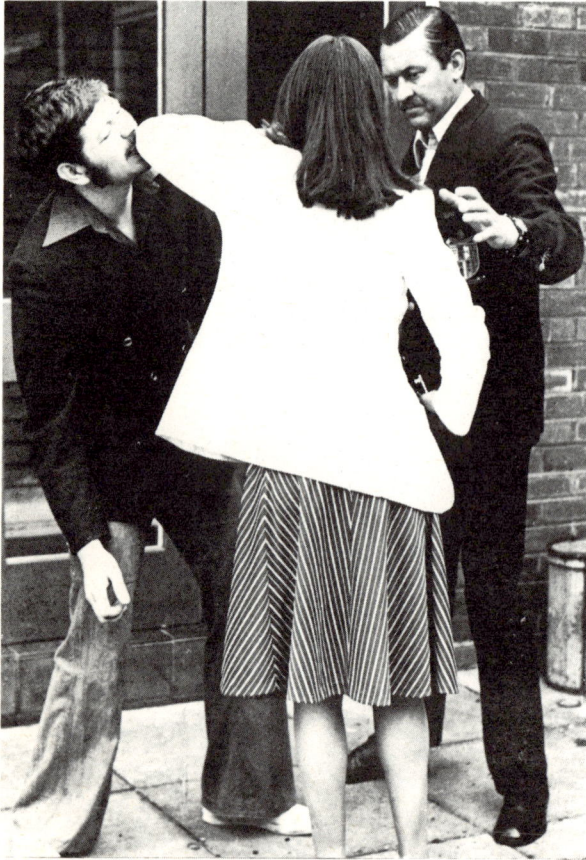

You have jabbed your elbow into the face of the nearest person. The lip is jammed between the elbow and teeth. This is your first and unexpected move. Your keys are held in your right hand prepared for your next attack.

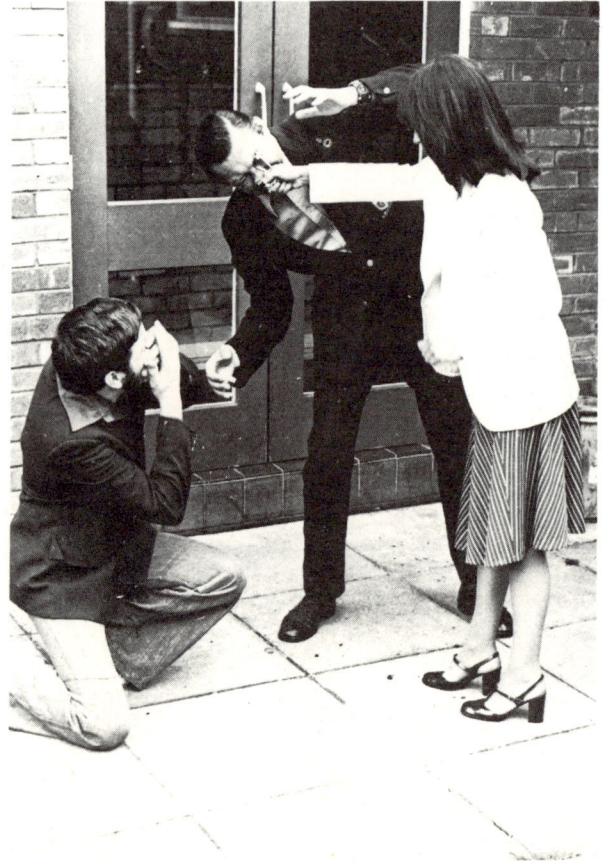

Push the keys into the nostrils or across the eyes of number two. You may have every reason to believe in the success of this movement as this person's attention would have been temporarily focused on the man with the sore lip.

A full swinging kick in between the legs of the next man should give you number three.

The above techniques can obviously be used in an emergency, but they are shown to demonstrate that the woman can be quite capable of dealing with more than one aggressor.

Example 41

Some of the things which a woman often has readily available—umbrella, handbag, keys, cologne spray, brush, comb, scissors, hairpins—can become weapons with intelligent use. Some uses of the umbrella have already been described. The handbag is convenient to push into a person's nose.

N.B. Never swing an umbrella or handbag against someone as it will just not work.

Some illustrations are as follows;

Draw a comb sharply down your opponent's nose (lips, neck).

Stick a key behind the edge of the jaw (nose, teeth).

Grind a ring into the temple of the aggressor.

A skilful and intelligent use of the umbrella—bring the point sharply on the aggressor's toe.

Pencil or pen pushed sharply against the jawline.

The spray cologne or larger spray within reach. Avoid the temptation to go for the eyes as your manoeuvre is obvious and your opponent may shut his eyes instinctively or on purpose. You may inflict pain or injury to a greater degree than desired. Aim upwards to the nostrils which cannot close automatically and which will cause sufficient discomfort to enable you to get away in peace.

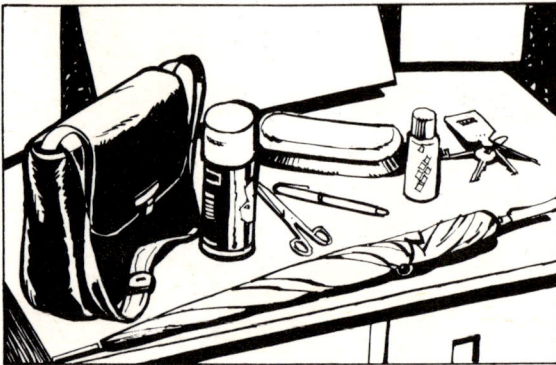

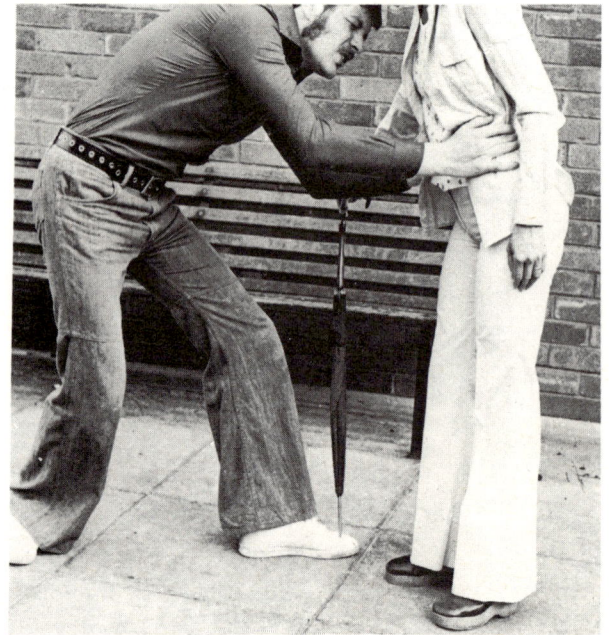

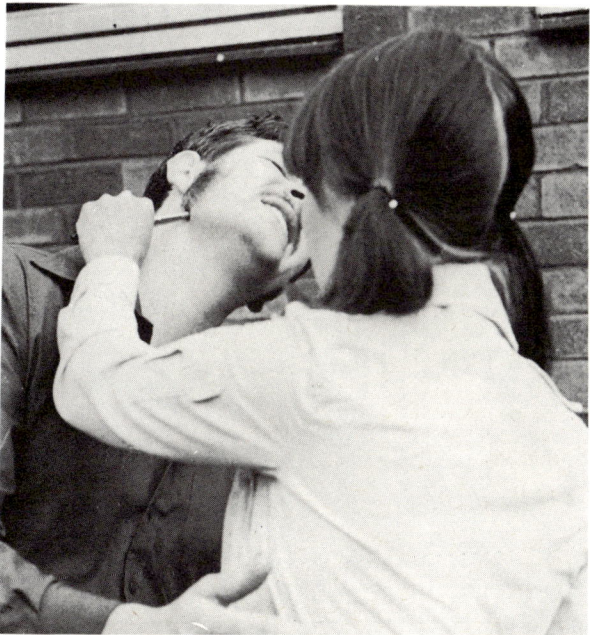
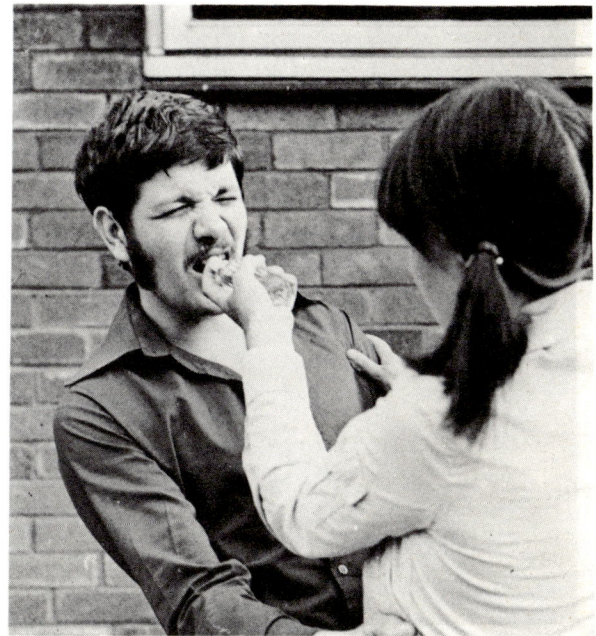

Example 42

You are making a telephone call from a public box. A man enters with violent intentions. An assault in this case can only occur when a girl is inside the box first. She has the telephone ledge protruding in front of her, glass panel walls on both sides, the fourth wall being made by the opponent pushing his way in. Attempting to push him out will commit her comparatively insignificant strength against a much stronger opponent.

As he commences his advance, cooperate sufficiently to enable you to half-turn so that the door is to your side. Establish close body contact. Put both arms on his shoulders gripping the material of his coat firmly. His face will instinctively move towards yours.

Using this movement pull firmly with your hands, at the last instant getting your head out of the way. The top of his head should come into violent contact with the side of the telephone box.

At this point, slide out through the door and get away or seek help.

Example 43

A man has entered your home and intends to rob you. Leaving him alone to go about his business may sometimes be preferable, as violence is regarded by many as the last resort and then only used in defence of oneself or others threatened by brutal aggression.

The man has just slapped your face and is pulling your hair. Clearly he wants to knock you about as well as take your possessions. Do not fight at random, work out your moves and apply them in rapid succession.

Strike a blow with your fist to the tip of his nose to cause a nosebleed, the fingers of your other hand pressing firmly downwards against his Adam's apple. Bring your knee up for the final blow. These attacks delivered accurately in rapid succession will give you enough time to get out and get help. Remember, get help outside.

Example 44

When someone breaks into your house with the clear intention of raping you, or you have been manoeuvred into a spare room at a party where you don't have the slightest intention of being seduced, you must allow him to get to close quarters and act decisively. You must bear in mind that any pain you may inflict might be considerably lessened by the intensity of his desire.

When close bodily contact has been established, with one hand pinch the soft skin inside his leg or his testicle, whichever is nearer to hand. With the second hand push, fingers extended like a claw, into his face. You do not wish to blind him for life so the main pressure directed upwards and to the rear is exerted on the sensitive tip of his nose by the upper palm of the hand. You have now hurt him in two places —in each case very sensitive places have been attacked.

If the door is at hand and you think you can get out of the house before he recovers, do so. If he is still barring the exit, pivot on one leg, support yourself on his shoulder and finish him off with your knee.

N.B. You have caused him an injury, not merely an inconvenience. At this stage if it seems too cruel, consider the following points;
a) That person forced his way into the room for the explicit purpose of raping you.
b) Words failed to dissuade him.
c) As an alternative to his injured pride and anatomy just think of the brutal consequences to yourself.

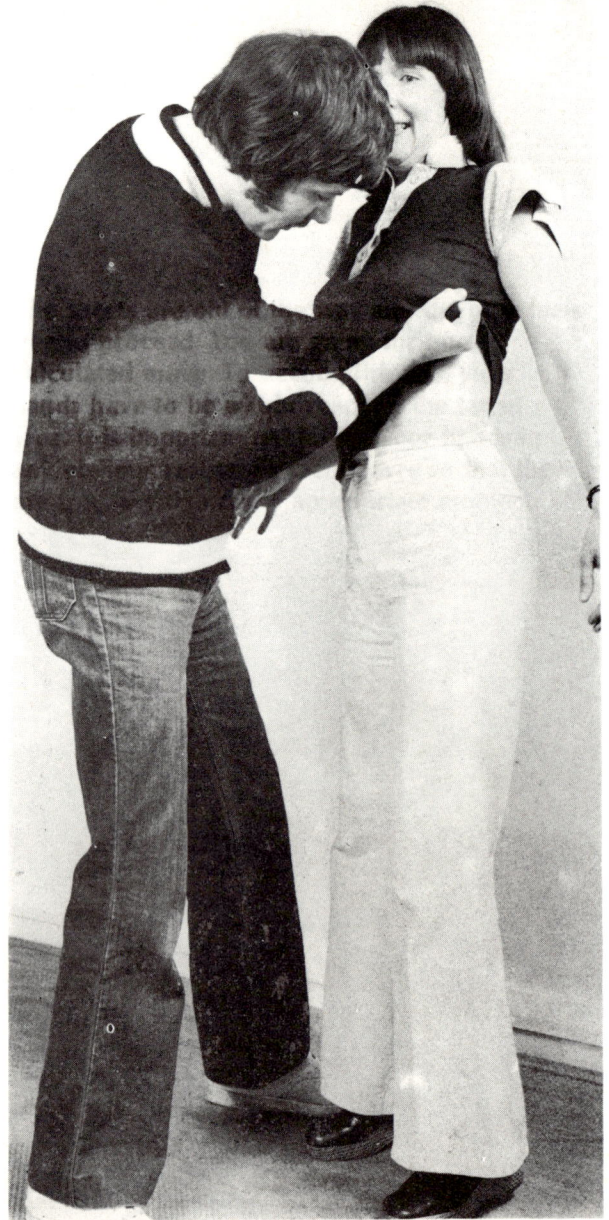

Example 45

A man breaks into your house and forces you towards your bed at knife-point. It is a question of submit or be stabbed. Look sufficiently frightened to make him think that his method is succeeding. Do not attempt to resist at this point.

Comply with his spoken or unspoken request. Once on the bed he will find the knife a handicap. Let him get on top of you. Do not resist but do not assist him. Lie in a passive state forcing him to take the sexual initiative.

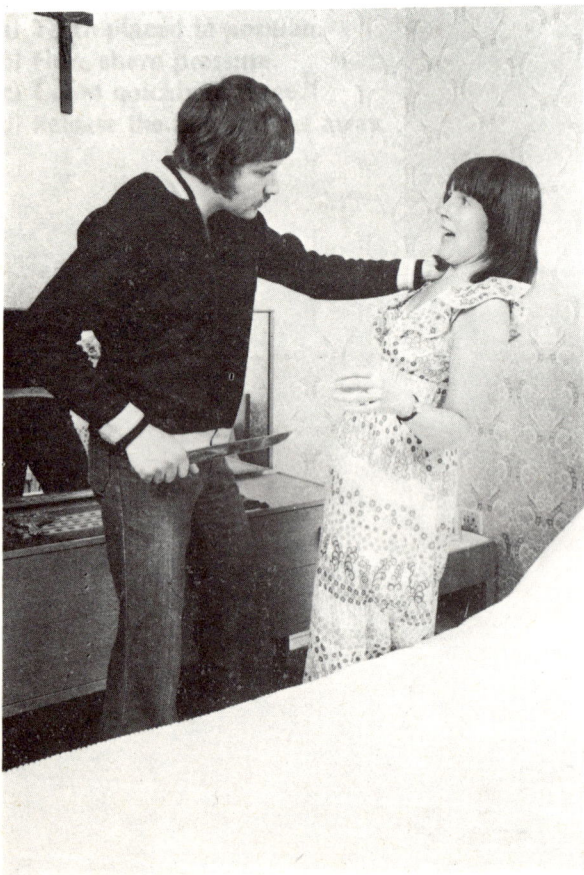

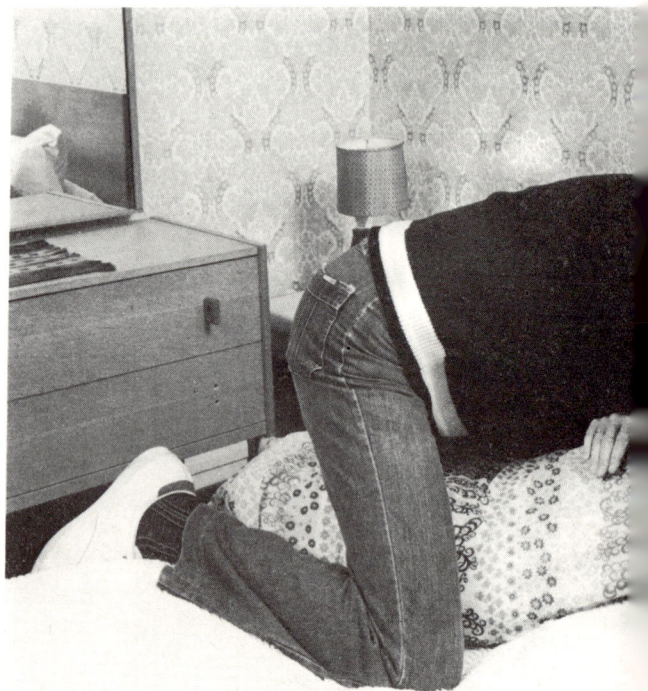

Sooner or later he will find the knife a nuisance as one hand left to him is not really adequate for further physical progress. When he feels reasonably secure and commits both hands, take hold of the knife and flick it away off the bed so that he may no longer have use of it.

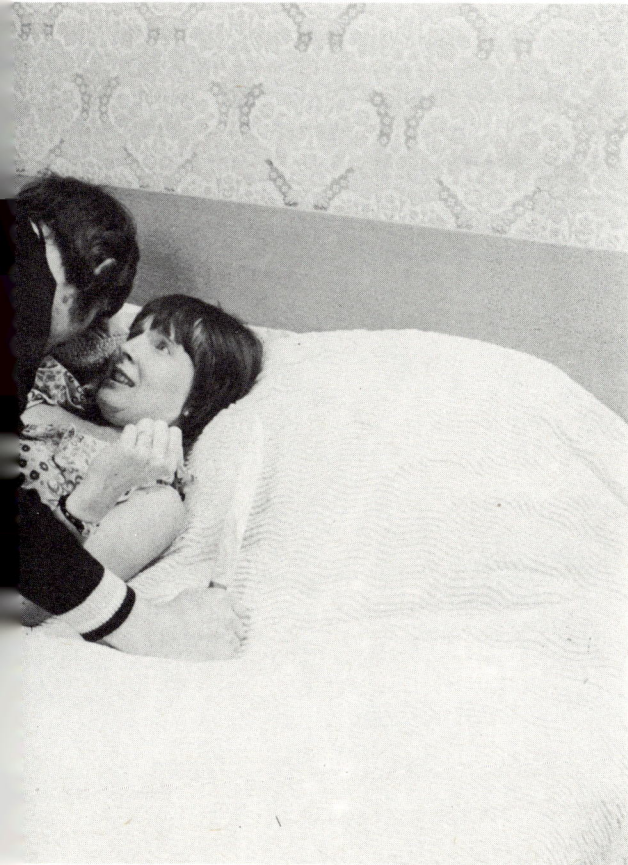

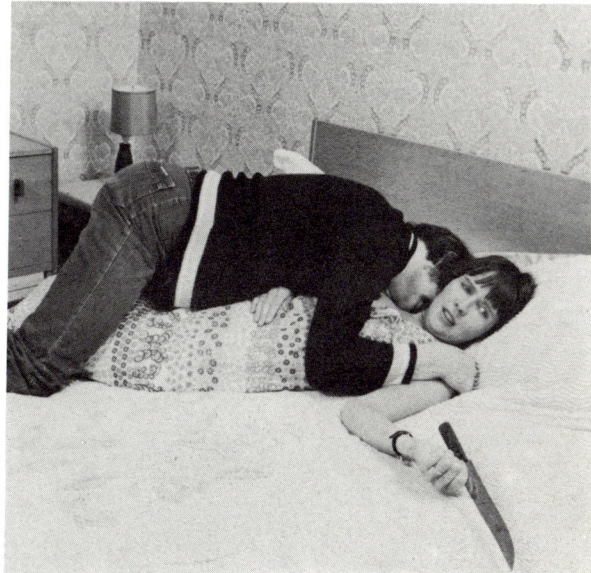

At this stage you have a man engrossed in his activity whose mind is fully committed to the task in hand, the knife is out of the way and you are in an ideal position to strike back as in the following example.

N.B. Whatever happens, do not attempt to use the knife as a weapon. You wish to disable the rapist in order to effect a getaway, not to indulge in a knife fight. Use your wit and your knowledge, not your strength or the knife.

Example 46

At this point I am trying to create a real-life situation where a girl is disturbed in bed by a man who has a specific desire to rape her at whatever cost.

You are in bed, covered by the sheet and blankets. A man is trying to rape you. Any resistance at this point would be useless. You are covered by the bedclothes and any struggling at this stage would only succeed in sapping your energy. Look suitably frightened and dismayed.

Let him fling the sheet and blankets off and let him proceed. Do not help—let him do all the work.

The sheets are out of the way and the man feels free to proceed. You are going for one calculated move. To accomplish this, your hands have to be within reach of the target area. It is important not to use your hands in any obvious resistance manoeuvre so that they are free to strike at the appropriate moment.

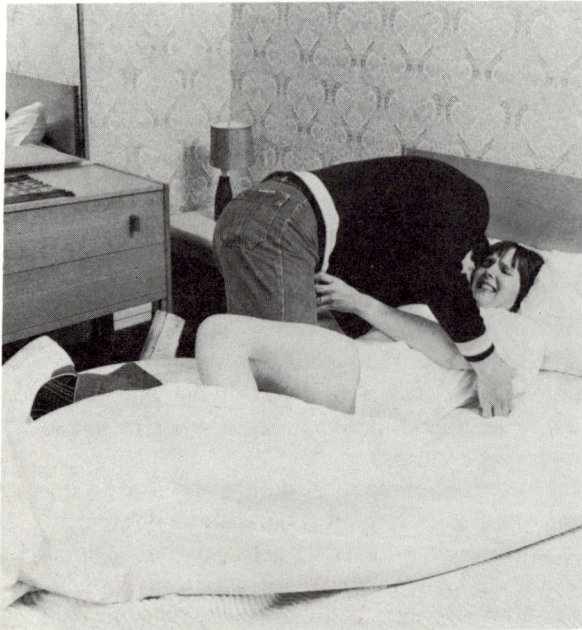

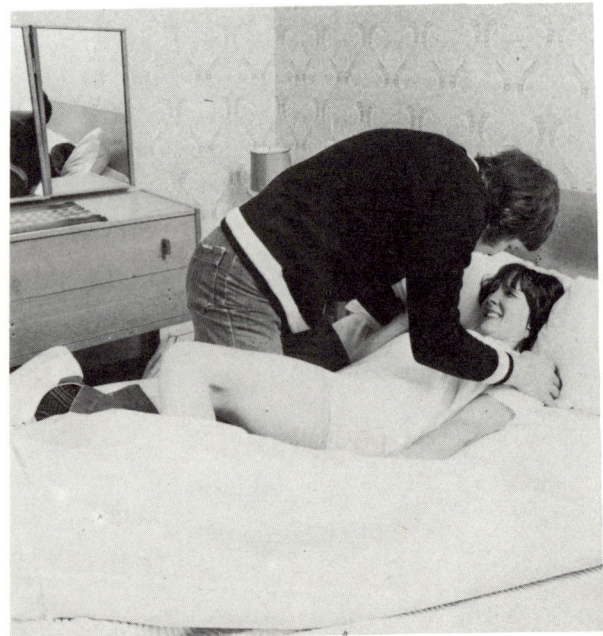

This is the moment of decision. You will either hurt the man or be raped by him. Assuming that you do not wish to be raped, when the man's lower abdomen is immediately above yours and your arms through lack of positive resistance are free, grab hold of his testicles, squeeze and jerk. This should cause him sufficient pain to enable you to roll out and get away. Do the only sensible thing possible, get out while he is still incapable of pursuit, leave the room and premises and seek help outside.

N.B. Do not attempt to use the telephone to summon help. You do not know the extent of his injuries and you do not wish to be attacked a second time. Switch the lights on, leave the doors wide open and phone from the nearest house where you know there is someone inside.

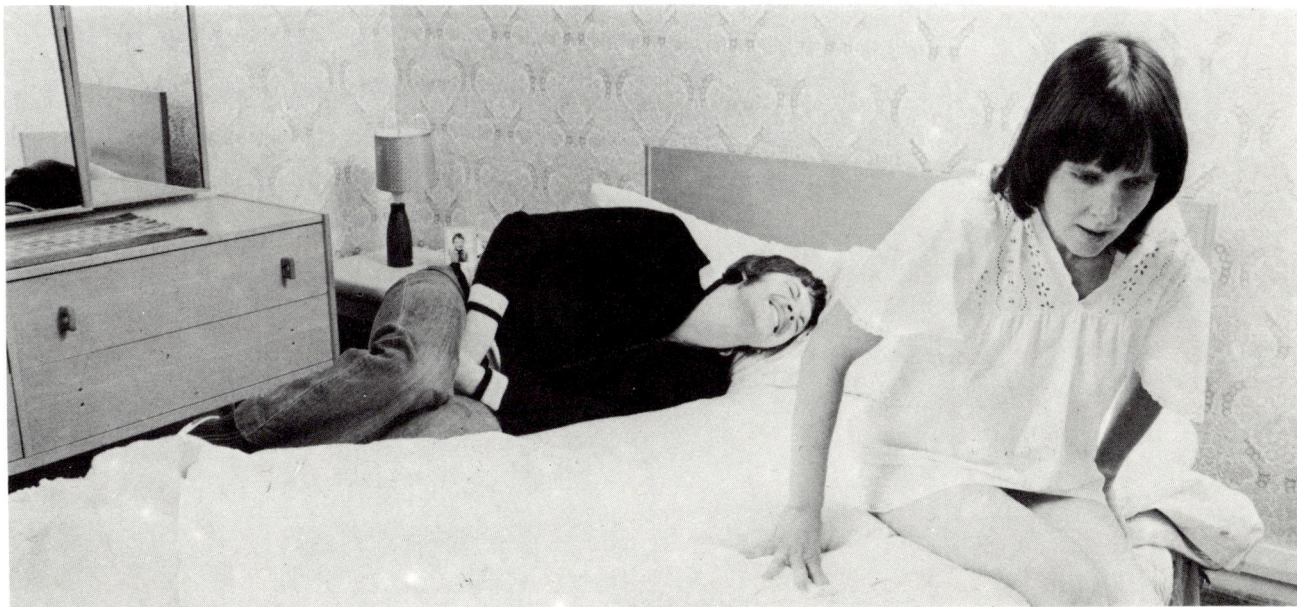

Example 47

Unfortunately, a pregnant woman is not safe from attack.
There are many defences a pregnant woman can employ against an attacker.

**At very close quarters you should be able to place your teeth on your attacker's Adam's apple so that it is firmly held. Exert sufficient pressure to make him let go of you and to choke and splutter. This will enable you to escape.
Do not prolong the bite as it can prove lethal.**

Suggested sequence;
a) Teeth placed in position.
b) Firm, sharp pressure.
c) Count quickly to three.
d) Release the bite and get away.

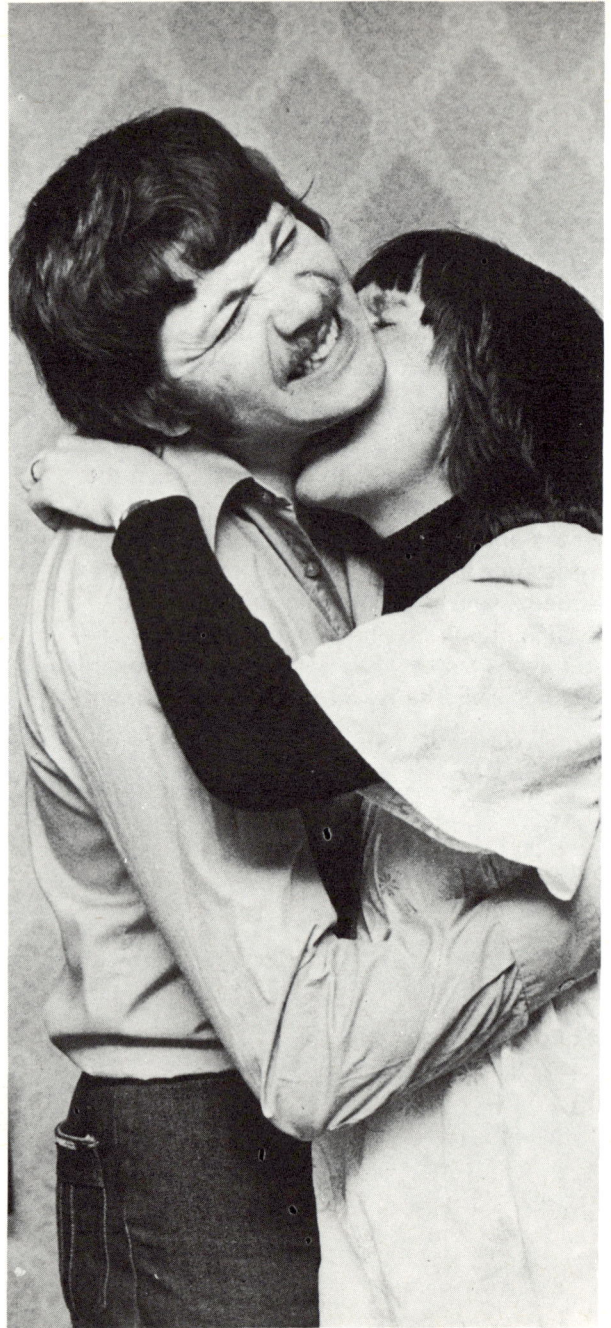

Example 48

A sharp bite to the corner of the jaw when the Adam's apple is out of reach and when struggling would result should an attempt be made to reach it. The pressure is exerted mainly on the underpart of the bone as the lower teeth are pushed sharply upwards. If necessary, this can be followed by pushing your elbow into his nose and eye.

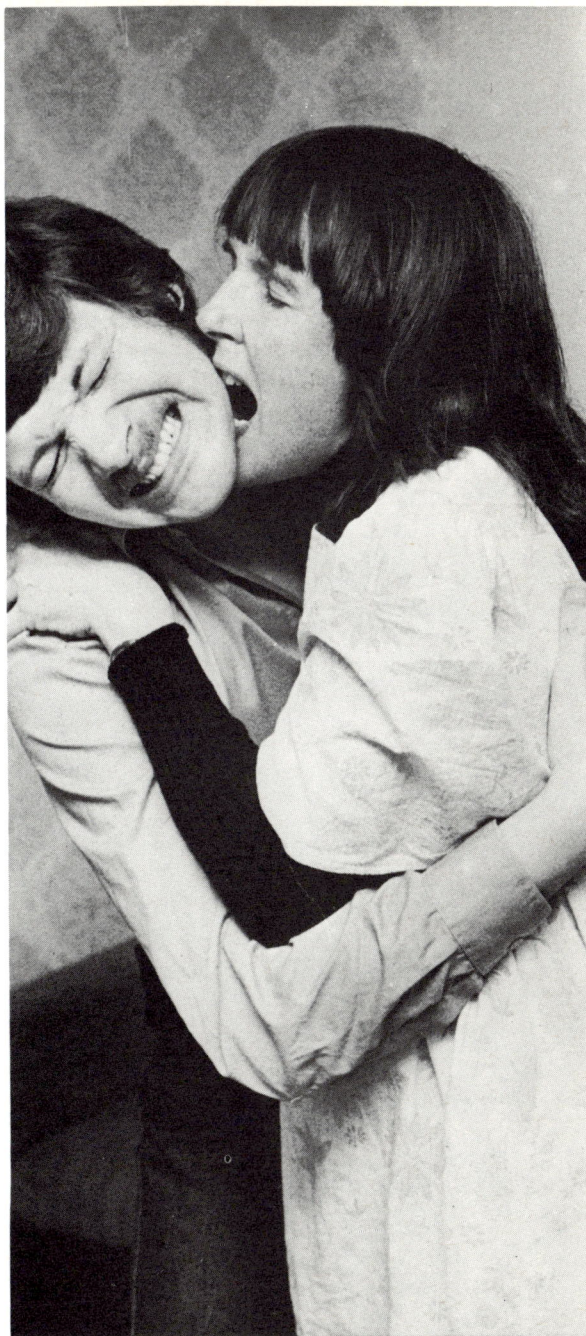

Example 49

If you are attacked while sitting in an armchair, with your assailant coming at you from above, do not attempt to struggle up and get caught half way.

Let him come close enough to;
a) Place both hands on his temples for stability.
b) Then press both your thumbs upwards in the corners formed by the top of the eyeball and just above. Your thumbs are above the eyelids and pressure is simultaneous on both sides.

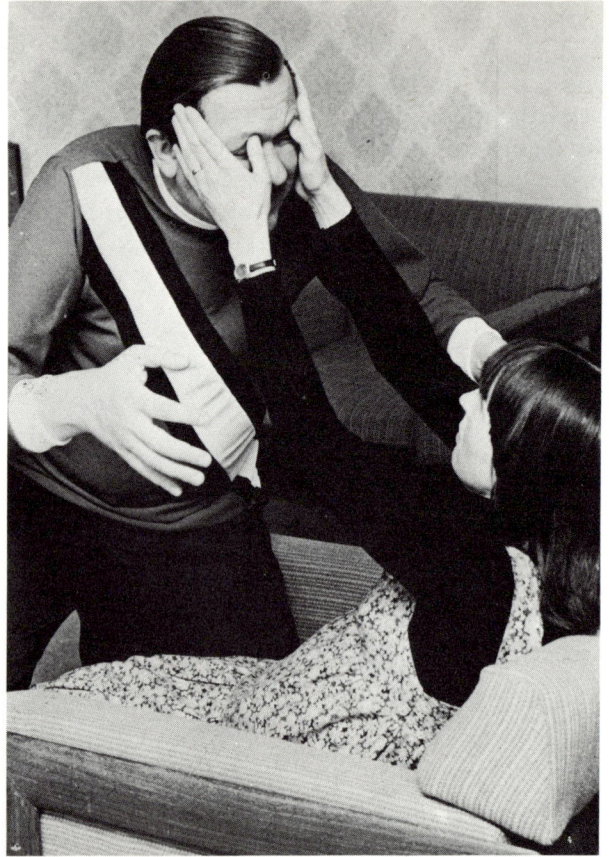

c) Ease yourself out between his legs and the arms of the chair as he reacts to the pain inflicted.

d) If he seems likely to come at you again, bring your elbow into his ear with the full weight of your body behind it.

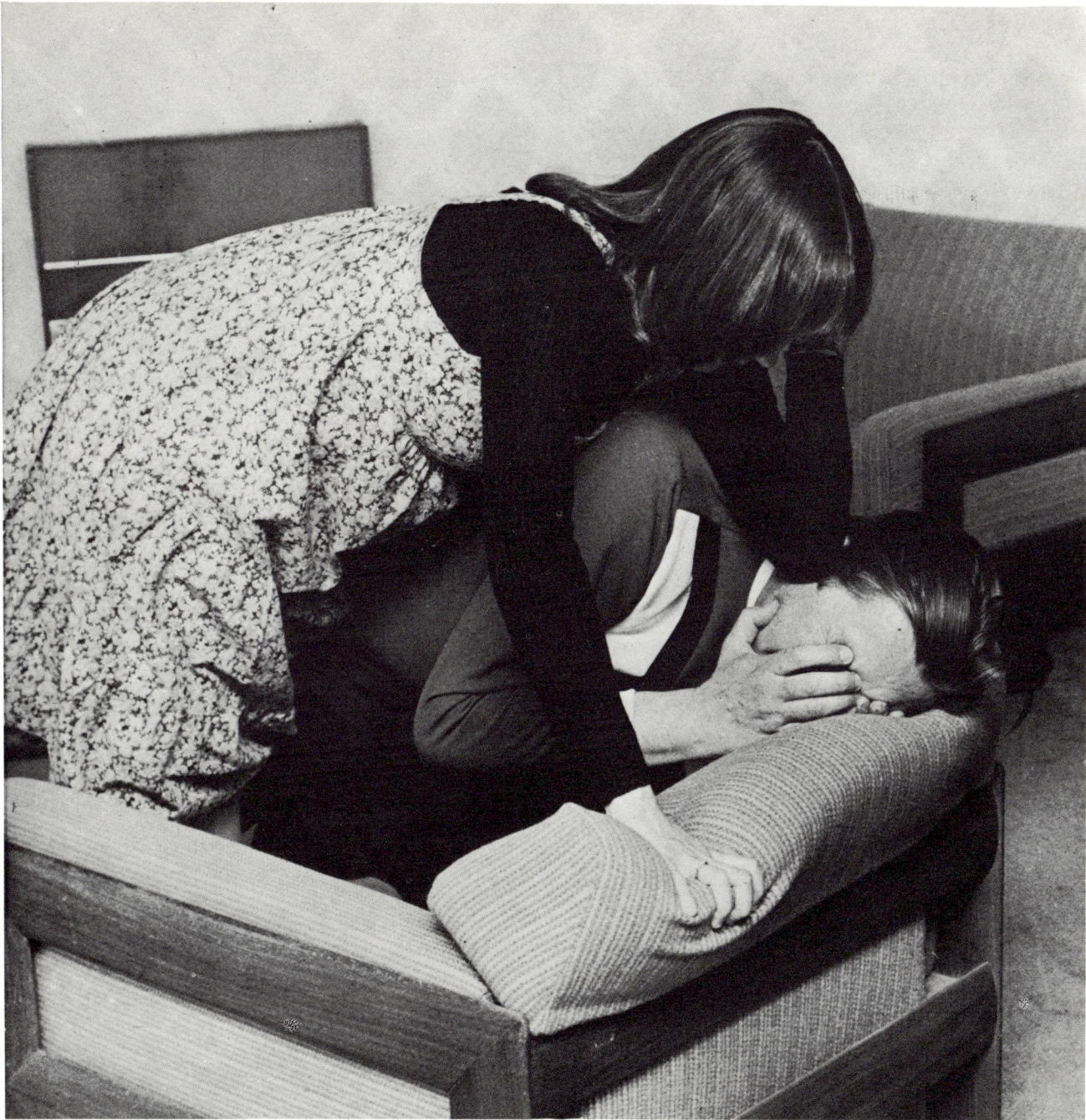

Example 50

If you are attacked by a woman, for any reason, she will spare nothing, using her arms, legs, teeth and nails in a tigress-like manner. You must apply a short sharp technique in order to gain time to remove yourself—do not attempt to argue with her.

Attack with the flat of your hand to her ear. This should give you a few seconds start.

Fingers forming a claw, attacking simultaneously the breathing apparatus and nerve centres on either side of the collar bone. The attack should consist of one sharp downward and inward movement of the fingertips. Disengage and disappear.

Curve the tips of your fingers well up. Side step quickly and attack upwards and inwards under your opponent's breast. This should render her sufficiently winded for you to be able to get away.

Form your hands so that the thumb is on the little finger leaving your other three fingers protruding forwards. Jab the fingers on both sides of the neck as shown in the photograph. The direction of the thrust follows an imaginary line which would enable your fingertips to meet should the continuation be possible. While the attacking woman is suffering the effects get away quickly.

As a last resort flick the tips of your fingers across your opponent's eyes.

All these situations are designed to give you sufficient time to leave the scene very quickly rather than pressing the attack home. Use the few seconds you will gain in these examples to make a quick exit.